MODERN
NATIONS
OF THE
WORLD

PANAMA

BY DAVID M. ARMSTRONG

LUCENT BOOKS

An imprint of Thomson Gale, a part of The Thomson Corporation

THOMSON

GALE

Detroit • New York • San Francisco • San Diego • New Haven, Conn. • Waterville, Maine • London • Munich

LIBRARY OF CONGRESS CATALOGING-IN-PUBLICATION DATA

Armstrong, David M., 1977-
    Panama / by David M. Armstrong.
p. cm. —(Modern nations of the world)
Includes bibliographical references and index.
    ISBN 1-59018-119-0 (hard cover : alk. paper)
    1. Panama—Juvenile literature. I. Title. II. Series.
F1563.2.A76 2005
972.87--dc22

2004010558

CONTENTS

INTRODUCTION

A LAND WITH MANY NAMES

The Isthmus of Panama, the Republic of Panama, the colony of Darién, Castillo del Oro, the Protectorate of Panama, the Path Between the Seas—Panama has been called many things in its long life. And it has meant many things to many people. It has changed with the centuries, just as its inhabitants have. But Panama's importance to the world has remained unchanged.

In its prehistoric days, the isthmus acted as a land bridge between the Americas, providing animals and peoples with a route of biological and cultural exchange. Later, as tribes began to move north from what is now Colombia into its territories, the isthmus became for them a source of food and refuge. Its more than five hundred rivers led early peoples to build canoes in order to traverse the land.

Then, when Europeans arrived, the isthmus took on a new identity: a barricade blocking European traders from their ultimate goal, the Asian trading ports of the Orient. The isthmus also turned out to be a gold mine. For the next three hundred years, Spain and its adversaries plundered the small strip of land. Then, as they stripped its people and countryside of its wealth, the Spanish used the isthmus as a place from which to launch their ships, which carried riches they had stolen from indigenous tribes and kingdoms in the north and south.

For nearly three hundred years, Panama remained a Spanish settlement whose resources and people were exploited. When America led the new age of industry right through the heart of Panama, first by rail, then by sea, the country once again filled with life and activity. But, as so often is the case, the triumph of one human endeavor leads to the travesty of another, and throughout the twentieth century Panama was plunged into a tumultuous time period featuring tyrants, revolutions, and schemers.

The Panama of today has nonetheless survived, and it has emerged as a rich, culturally diverse place. It has a thriving business sector in which the nations of the world come to trade. It is a crossroads for ships traveling from the Pacific to the Atlantic and a passageway from North to South America. It is a tourist spot where international travelers come to enjoy some of nature's most beautiful places in the world. It is said that Panama means "abundance of fish." Today, it also means an abundance of culture, history, and peoples; but no matter what name it goes by, Panama is a place not soon forgotten.

AN OLD MAN AT THE BEGINNING OF HIS LIFE

The rich and troubled history of Panama is built into its modern character. Centuries of strife, war, devastation, conquest, and exploration pervade all aspects of Panamanian life. Indeed, Panama is still healing from the attempts by tyrannical dictators like Manuel Noriega to take advantage of

Pictured is the skyline of Panama City with fishing boats in the harbor. Despite its tumultuous history, Panama is today a democratic nation with a strong economy.

its people and resources. Slowly, however, Panamanians have gained a voice by becoming a democratic nation.

Other problems still persist, however. The natural biological diversity of Panama's dense rain forests is constantly threatened by ecologically hazardous farming techniques. Likewise, growing urban sectors encroach upon and endanger the natural habitats of thousands of plant and animal species. Racism and poverty continue to plague rural and urban areas alike. Economic challenges likely lay ahead: While the Panama Canal made the country part of the world economy, its future may be in question as many newer ships are too large to pass through the canal. Panama also must contend with a looming drug trafficking problem. And while the military dictatorships that once ruled Panama have been replaced with democracy, corruption threatens to spoil the freedom for which its citizens have fought.

Panama is thus like an old man who has lived a long life with many experiences, but now faces the proposition of entering into a new phase as if he had just been born. This is the Panama of today, a concoction of the old and the new, building upon its past while looking to overcome its problems for a brighter future.

A WORLD UNTO ITSELF

Panama is located in Central America. It is an isthmus, a piece of land connecting the two larger landmasses of North and South America. This relatively small, S-shaped country —slightly smaller than South Carolina—is only about thirty-one miles wide at its narrowest point, making it the thinnest strip of land separating the Atlantic and Pacific oceans. But Panama is more than a mere land bridge.

The nineteenth-century general Simón Bolívar once noted, "If the world had to choose a capital, the Isthmus of Panama would be the obvious place for that high destiny."[1] And, in fact, this tiny crossway of the world has played its role as a center of activity for the Western Hemisphere since volcanic activity pushed the land up from beneath the ocean

PANAMA

almost 3 million years ago. Panama—with its two mountain ranges, 765 miles of Pacific coast, 425 miles of coast along the Caribbean, and nearly five hundred rivers—has served as a central gathering place for hundreds of species of reptiles, insects, and mammals (including humans), not to mention a repository for more than 10,000 species of plant life. Panama also shelters about 960 bird species.

Panama's variant geography and development have made it a country of distinct geographic regions. These regional differences have produced an intense variety of animals, plant life, climates, terrains, and islands.

PANAMA PROVINCE

The province of Panama is one of the country's most inhabited provinces as well as its main center of activity. Panama Province is home to nearly half of the country's population—a population that is quite diversified. The Panama Canal is located in this province, and so peoples from all over the world are drawn here for both trade and tourism. According to author Peter Eltringham, "North American cultural influence, though strong, is but one among many [in Panama Province]. Spanish, African, West Indian, Chinese, Indian, European [all make for] a compelling cultural mix, creating perhaps the most . . . outward-looking society in Central America."[2]

Panama Province is also home to Panama City, the nation's capital. Panama City is an intriguing mix of old and new. To the east is the site where the city was originally founded, called Old Panama. All that remains of this city, the first Spanish settlement on the Pacific, are stone ruins. The pirate Henry Morgan burned the whole town to the ground in 1671. After that, the city was moved west a few miles. The area where the city was rebuilt is called various names—the Old Part, the Ancient Part, or simply the San Felipe district. San Felipe has become run-down, and the center of the city has moved farther west toward the canal. Here, in Punta Paitilla, skyscrapers and modern city streets make up the bustling business district. Just northwest of here is the Metropolitan Natural Park, a 655-acre park within the city containing an ecoregion (a large piece of land made up of a specific kind of natural habitat) known as the Lowland Pacific Forest, which is home to 45 mammal, 36 reptile, 14 amphibian, and 227 bird species.

PANAMA'S NATIONAL PARKS

Sixteen national parks cover nearly 22 percent of Panama, and each one hosts a wide array of animal and plant life. The Altos de Campana National Park sits inside Panama Province, and is home to the famous golden frogs that ancient Indians believed could turn into real gold and bring good fortune. In Bastimentos Island National Marine Park, manatees (sea cows) and sea turtles swim among coral reefs with over two hundred species of marine fish. In Las Cruces National Park live two- and three-toed sloths and howler monkeys.

Perhaps the best example of the diversity within Panama's national parks is the Barro Colorado Nature Monument. At the center of Gatún Lake is Barro Colorado Island, which was a hill until the creation of the lake caused only the top of the hill to be above water. Countless animals flocked to the top, creating a dense concentration of diverse life. More than two hundred species of ants inhabit the island, and it is home to a silk cotton tree that has been named "Big Tree" because it is so large that other trees grow in its branches.

The nature monument is home to 5 species of monkey: howlers, spider monkeys, marmosets, capuchins, and night monkeys. There are nearly 60 species of bats and 384 species of birds in the rain forest, including the crested guan and the great tinamou. This rain forest is not without its reptiles and amphibians: 47 species of snakes live there, along with 22 species of lizards and 30 species of frogs. Scientists estimate that there are around 300 species of butterflies and 200 ant species, including 14 different kinds of army ants.

Many of Panama's parks are threatened by logging and farming, which cut and burn trees of the rain forest to make room for cattle grazing. Las Cruces, like many other parks, is also in trouble because of its proximity to the ever-expanding Panama City. While tourism has helped to fund these parks, tourism has also hastened the urban expansion of cities such as Panama City, Santiago, and David, which have been increasing in size and population at high rates since the 1950s.

The three-toed sloth is unique to the tropical jungles of Central and South America.

A kayaker paddles toward one of Panama's Pearl Islands. These islands have many lagoons in which pearl-providing oysters live.

Just twelve miles south of Panama City are ten Pacific islands that are also part of Panama Province. The largest of these is Taboga, a small island in the middle of the gulf where pirates used to stay between raids. The island has become one of Panama's most popular tourist spots. It is home to the Taboga Island Wildlife Refuge, where tourists can see blue morpho butterflies, lizards, and many bird species along the Cerro de las Tres Cruces Trail, which leads to the top of the island and offers visitors views of many of the other islands. Moray eels, hammerhead sharks, orcas, humpback whales, marlin, dolphins, and manta rays have all been known to inhabit the waters around the island. In fact, the island's original name, Aboga, meant "Many Fish."

Other islands belonging to the province include Contadora, a popular tourist spot known for its beautiful beaches and palm trees; San José, which is almost nothing but solid rain forest; and the Pearl Islands, a string of islands known for their lagoons in which pearl-producing oysters live. Some of the world's most exquisite pearls come from this region, including the famous Peregrina pearl. This incredible pearl is about the size of a pigeon's egg.

Colón Province

About fifty miles north of Panama City is the province of Colón. Colón Province, and its capital city, also named Colón, are home to one of the world's greatest areas of commerce and industry. The Atlantic end of the Panama Canal is at Colón, which means that its harbors are constantly full of international freighters carrying goods from all over the world. Colón has been a center of activity since the Spanish landed there over four hundred years ago, when a haggard explorer demanded that his party stop to take a rest from the jungle and harsh climate. Ironically, nothing has stopped moving since in the province of Colón.

Colón is most famous for its *zona libre*, or free-trade zone. A center of international industry and commercial trade, the zone is a twelve-hundred-acre steel-and-concrete complex in which more than sixteen hundred companies and two dozen banks do business, making it the second-largest free-trade zone in the world, second only to Hong Kong. Sadly though, not much of the money changing hands in the free-trade zone transfers to the community. This is because almost all of the business is conducted between companies within the complex. Only a small portion of the surrounding population is included in this commerce, and these Colón inhabitants are usually part of the service sector working to maintain the complex, such as janitors, security guards, and port workers. As a result, several surrounding towns, such as Escobal, are some of the poorest urban communities in Panama.

Colón, however, is not all concrete and steel. Gatún Lake, which stretches over the provinces of Panama and Colón, is located at the northern end of the Panama Canal. When it was formed in 1914, it was the largest man-made lake in the world, measuring 163 square miles. It held this title until the creation of Lake Mead in Nevada in 1935. Gatún Lake was created as a result of the Gatún Dam, whose construction on the Chagres River in conjunction with the Panama Canal flooded twenty-nine villages, displacing roughly fifty thousand people.

Coclé Province

West of Panama Province and south of Colón sits Coclé Province. Within Coclé Province, nestled in the upper reaches of the Cordillera Central (a mountain range) sits the small village of El Valle de Anton. Over 2.5 million years ago a volcano exploded here with such force that it blew its top off, leaving nothing but a crater. In the crater there formed a lake, which eventually spilled over from a break in its side and drained. A large amount of fertile soil had settled in the bottom of the crater, so when humans came into the area, they found that this soil provided excellent farming ground. The town of El Valle sprang up here.

Because of its altitude (about two thousand feet above sea level), the cool climate, and the fertile soil formation, the farmers of El Valle are able to grow delicate fruits and vegetables that are difficult to maintain in the hotter climates below, such as tomatoes and strawberries. Also because of these unique traits, El Valle is home to many delicate wild flowers, including orchids. El Valle is most famous for producing a white orchid called the holy ghost, Panama's national flower.

El Valle has become a popular tourist spot for visitors to Panama for these reasons and others. Not only is it a cooler

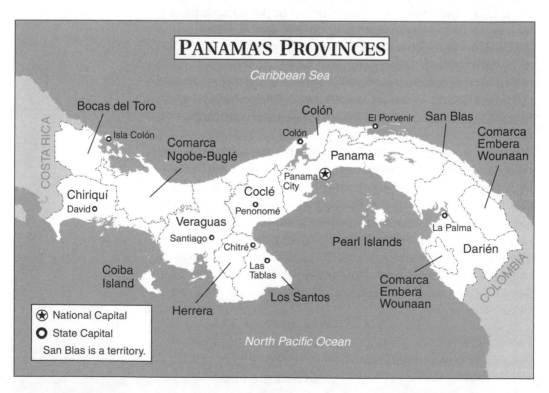

and less humid area than the lower lands of Coclé Province, but other attractions also make it unique. Among them are thermal baths that are heated from hot springs near the Anton River. There are the odd-looking *arboles quadrados*, or "Square Trees," named because their trunks do not grow round but instead have four flat sides. There are also golden frogs, which have become the unofficial mascots of El Valle. A popular activity in El Valle is to go looking for these one-inch long, yellow, black-spotted frogs in the rain forests surrounding the towns. But to the untrained eye, the frogs can be very elusive. Fortunately for tourists, there are some frogs on display at a small zoo where they are kept behind mesh screens, which is safer for everyone since these frogs are poisonous.

THE HERRERA, LOS SANTOS, AND VERAGUAS PROVINCES

West of El Valle and Coclé are the Herrera, Los Santos, and Veraguas provinces, all of which make up the Azuero Peninsula. The Azuero (meaning "adze," another name for an axe) Peninsula, the southern tip of central Panama that juts out into the Pacific Ocean, received its name because it resembles the head of an axe or hatchet.

The Caribbean coast of Veraguas (also known as the Mosquito Coast for the Mosquito Gulf) is thick with vegetation and dense rain forest. Many parts of this area can only be reached by boat. To the south, however, the climate is less humid, so more people have settled here. The people here have brought with them the lucrative business of industrial logging. Many also began raising cattle and cleared much of the land for grazing. By settling here and logging the land, people have destroyed almost 95 percent of the rain forests that once covered the peninsula. Because of this, much of the Azuero Peninsula has become dry farmland and desert.

Despite the logging and settlements, the peninsula is still home to Panamanian dry forests that serve as homes for many migratory birds and other animals. Dry forests consist of certain kinds of trees that require only half as much rainfall as tropical rain forests but can still thrive in the heat of tropical lowland climates. Dry forests once covered more than two hundred thousand square miles of coastal lowland areas along the Pacific Ocean from Panama all the way into central Mexico. The dry forests, which now cover an area of only around two thousand square miles, roughly the size of Delaware, are also being threatened by increased burning and logging for cattle ranching. And because the trees held the valuable topsoil in place and kept moisture in the soil, their absence has allowed topsoil and vital nutrients to wash away into the ocean. Between 2002 and 2003, Panama experienced a bad drought that lasted for almost a year. Cattle ranchers began losing their livestock because grass no longer grew. Farmers lost crops because there was no moisture in the soil. Only then did some people realize the value of the dry forests. Environmentalists just hope it is not too late to save what is left.

THE CHIRIQUÍ AND BOCAS DEL TORO PROVINCES

Continuing west are the provinces of Chiriquí and Bocas del Toro. Most of the province of Chiriquí sits comfortably amid the Cordillera Central mountain range, which stretches nearly 250 miles to the Costa Rican border. Because of their altitudes in the mountains, many areas of Chiriquí Province are cooler and less humid than other lower-lying lands in Panama. However, the capital, David, is humid and hot all year because it is lower and nearer the ocean. Nonetheless, this capital, which is Panama's third-largest city with nearly seventy-eight thousand people, is a rich farming community. For decades, many towns around David have specialized in growing bananas, selling much of their crops to the internationally famous Chiquita banana company.

To the northwest of David sits Barú volcano, the highest point in Panama at 11,401 feet, and Panama's only volcano (though it has not erupted for more than five hundred years). Barú is a popular vacationing spot for tourists because of its cooler climate and its vast scenery of orange groves and tropical forest canopy. In fact, from the top of Barú on a clear day, a person can see both the Atlantic and Pacific oceans. The surrounding national park affords visitors the chance to test their hiking skills on some of the steepest trails in Panama.

The province of Bocas del Toro lies directly north of Chiriquí and borders Costa Rica on the west. Across this border spans Amistad International Park. *Amistad* means "friendship." The park got its unique name because it was created jointly by the Costa Rican and Panamanian

The Life of a Coiba Prisoner

Three hours by boat off the Panamanian coast in the Gulf of Chiriquí sits the 192-square-mile Coiba Island. Coiba, Panama's largest island, is unique in a way perhaps no other island in the world is. It is both a national park and a federal prison, the world's largest island prison. Coiba Prison sits within a 1,053-square-mile nature preserve, over 80 percent of which is oceanic and surrounds the island, complete with a mangrove forest and alligators.

Because the island is practically nothing but jungle, most Coiba prisoners are not confined to the large cement detention building called simply "Central." They are allowed to roam the island at will, and a few are even made tourist guides. Scott Doggett, in the travel guidebook *Panama*, writes about the prisoners and their jobs: "Eight to 10 model prisoners are allowed to work . . . preparing meals, washing clothes, and even leading tourists on snorkeling jaunts in the cove. Most are killers who've been on the island for many years and have earned the trust of the guards. . . . About half the convicts at the [park] station have pets—among them a very friendly deer, a scarlet macaw . . . and Volvo, a happy black dog with a white paw whose owner stole Swedish-made cars."

At night, the guards lock themselves into the guard huts along with their weapons. In the morning, there is a roll call. If a prisoner is absent from this activity, he is considered escaped, and if he returns or is caught, a two- to three-year extension is added to his sentence. A second attempt will result in a sentencing for life. A large number of the escapees return days later, dehydrated and haggard from being lost in the jungle, having no way off the island or enough survival skills to make it on their own. Despite these challenges, rumors abound that some escaped prisoners are actually eking out an existence deep within the jungle.

An armed prison guard stands watch at Panama's federal prison on Coiba Island.

A plantation worker harvests a bunch of bananas destined for export. Many residents of the province of Bocas del Toro are involved in the banana industry.

governments. The park is divided almost equally between the two countries and protects over three hundred bird species and over ninety mammal species, including giant anteaters, the Baird's tapir, and all six species of tropical cat: the jaguar, puma, ocelot, margay, oncilla, and jaguarundi. Among those who also call the park home are two indigenous Indian tribes, the Guaymi and the Teribe. These two tribes share much of the vast park with another tribe, the Bribri Indians, who are indigenous to Costa Rica.

Another important part of Bocas del Toro Province is the chain of islands off its coast. The Bocas del Toro Archipelago consists of six large islands, covered almost completely in forest, and hundreds of tiny islands with nothing but mangrove trees. Mangrove trees are tropical trees that are especially adapted to growing in and around saltwater and even have roots that hold the trees above water. Their roots are especially visible at low tide. These islands are so thick with vegetation that only one, Colón Island, has roads. The weather in this region is extremely rainy, but the archipelago is perfect for many nonhuman inhabitants. Eight species of sea turtle exist in the world, and four of them frequent this island chain. The green, hawksbill, leatherback, and logger-head sea turtles all find a resting place in the sands here for their precious eggs. In addition, the tiny rock island Little Swan Cay is the only place in Panama where the red-billed tropic bird (*Phaethon aethereus*) is known to nest.

Darién Province and Comarca de San Blas

Eastern Panama is a lush, rich land thick with dense rain forest, but it may not stay this way for long. Industrialization and urbanization are increasingly spreading into the jungle and tropical forests in the east. Indigenous peoples inhabit this region. The Comarca de San Blas is an autonomous (self-governed) region held by the Kuna Indians that is located north of Darién on the border of Colombia. The densely forested Darién Province, which also borders Colombia, is home to both the Embera and the Wounaan indigenous tribes.

Shady Dealing

About thirty-three hundred feet above sea level, in the Cordillera Central mountain range, sits the town of Boquete. This little town, which is just a few blocks long, is a place of distinct smells. Boquete is best known for its flowers, its orange groves, and, most of all, its coffee.

A light, foggy drizzle present in Boquete helps to maintain premium conditions for coffee growth, which the local plantations grow to the highest standards in all respects. For this reason, coffee plantations in Boquete such as Café Ruiz are not only known worldwide for the taste of their coffee but for their way of growing it as well.

The coffee bushes in Boquete are shade-grown, which means that instead of cutting down forests to plant fields of coffee, which can lead to erosion and force a higher use of pesticide to keep bugs away, they are planted beneath rows of trees. Oftentimes, these trees are the orange trees for which Boquete is also famous. Shade-growing coffee is a recommended method among naturalists because the trees protecting the coffee plants also provide much-needed homes for various species of wildlife, particularly Panama's vast bird population. Boquete's preeminence in coffee, oranges, and flowers (lilies, statices, hibiscus, hortenses, anthuriums, roses, St. Josephs, carnations, sunflowers, and orchids) has earned it the name "Valley of Flowers and Eternal Spring" and has made it home to more than one festival celebrating its flowers and coffee.

Both regions are distinct. The San Blas Islands are an archipelago of almost four hundred islands, all within three miles of Panama's Caribbean coast. A strip of land runs for 140 miles along this northern coast. This strip and the archipelago make up the Comarca de San Blas and are home to nearly forty thousand Kuna Indians, the extreme majority of whom live mainly on forty of the larger islands.

Darién, on the other hand, is a vast province of mostly jungle stretching over nearly 6,500 square miles, with few inhabitants. Despite its largely untamed wilderness, within Darién is Lake Bayano, a man-made lake formed in 1972 by the building of the Bayano hydroelectric dam. The dam, which provides Panama City with most of its power, flooded approximately 135 square miles of tropical rain forest and displaced two thousand Kuna and five hundred Embera Indians in its formation.

THE DARIÉN GAP

Darién, the largest province in Panama, is as well known for what it is not as for what it is. A large section of Darién Province is known as the Darién Gap. The "gap" is a thick, lush stretch of jungle that has barely been penetrated by civilization. This is not, however, due to the fact that civilization has not tried to spread to the Darién Gap. Indeed, the Darién Gap resisted the construction of the Pan-American Highway (also known as the Interamericana), a highway system that connects all of North, Central, and South America. The Pan-American Highway was begun as an international project in the late 1920s, and it is now nearly finished except for the Darién Gap. The dense jungle of the Darién Gap is a ninety-three-mile break in the pavement of an otherwise unbroken nineteen-thousand-mile highway.

The gap also happens to be one of the most biologically diverse areas in the world. Birds such as the viridian dacnis, the barred puffbird, the tooth-billed hummingbird, and black-tipped cotinga call this jungle home, as do nearly three hundred other species. This makes it a popular destination for bird-watching enthusiasts from all over the world. Some nocturnal animals like the night monkey, kinkajou, and crested owl also live here. The endangered harpy eagle, Panama's national bird, is all but extinct everywhere else in Central America, but it still thrives in Darién. The harpy is the most powerful bird of prey in the world and can reach lengths of up to three feet from beak to tail with a wingspan of seven feet. These birds nest in various kinds of trees. Darién is a good home for them because it is made up of six different kinds of forest, including tropical dry forests, marshes and swamp forests, and the semi-deciduous tropical moist forest. This last group accounts for many of the larger trees in the rain forest, such as the *Bombacopsis quinata*, which is pollinated by bats and is used by natives to make furniture.

Darién is a huge source of debate between proponents of the Pan-American Highway and ecologists who are fighting

A harpy eagle looks out from its nest high in the trees. This endangered bird of prey is Panama's national bird.

to keep the jungles of Darién protected. These defenders of the Darién jungle do not want to see Darién undergo the same kind of development that has ravaged many other rain forest regions throughout Panama and Central America. At least for now, the ecologists have won because the Pan-American Highway turns into a small patch of mud where the blacktop ends at a tiny town called Yaviza.

Factors other than ecology have contributed to the unfinished highway. The indigenous Embera and Wounaan peoples inhabit the area, living off the very jungles that the highway threatens. Also, an outbreak of foot-and-mouth disease (a highly contagious disease that threatens healthy livestock but not humans) in South America made Panamanian officials hesitant to complete the road, fearing it would lead to an epidemic that would affect the country's ranching industry. Likewise, there is concern that the road would also open Panama to more serious drug trafficking from Colombia. And in addition to all of these concerns has been the sheer cost of clearing a swath of land through the untamed wilderness.

Darién, like the entire country of Panama, is a diverse and pristine place where, for now, nature continues to thrive alongside human settlement. It remains a vital component of a land that is built on variety. All different kinds of plants, climates, animals, and terrains combine to make a beautiful picture of the land known as Panama.

From Spain's Discovery to an International Passageway

The story of the modern nation of Panama begins with the dawn of the sixteenth century. The Americas were only just being discovered by Europeans. Seeking wealth, fame, and land, explorers began working their way along the coast of South America and had moved as far west as present-day Colombia. Portugal and Spain led the race in claiming land as their own, despite finding indigenous inhabitants, whom they mistakenly dubbed Indians (because they originally thought they had reached India). Thus, the word *Indian* came to be used in reference to all native American tribes. No one knew it yet, but Panama was about to become the central landing and shipping point for European explorers and settlers. The Europeans would invade and plunder nearly every piece of land from Mexico through South America. The face of the isthmus was about to change forever.

Spain's New Land

The Spanish were the first Europeans to explore Central and South America. In 1501 a wealthy Spanish explorer named Rodrigo de Bastidas followed the coast of South America up to what is now Panama, becoming the first European ever to see the isthmus. Then, in 1502, Christopher Columbus completed the exploration of Panama's coast. Columbus met the Guaymi, Indians who wore pure gold breastplates. Columbus and his men traded cheap bells for the golden breastplates and other golden items. Columbus later wrote, "I saw greater evidence of gold on the first two days [in Panama] than in four years in Hispaniola [an island in the West Indies to which Columbus had also been]."[3]

Upon his return to Spain in 1504, Columbus reported that

21

Christopher Columbus explored Panama in 1502. His reports of abundant gold in Panama led many Spanish settlers to migrate to the area.

a region of Panama called Veragua was rich in goldfields (districts rich enough in gold to be mined) even though he had little proof of this other than loot from the Indians. Afterward, the Spanish called most of what is now Panama by the name of Castillo del Oro, which means "Castle of Gold." The promise of riches attracted many Spanish entrepreneurs to the shores of Panama, so many that the Spanish court agreed to establish a Spanish colony there.

Diego de Nicuesa, Castillo del Oro's first governor, arrived from Spain in 1509 with seven hundred men, but his time there was disastrous. After becoming shipwrecked near a place named Belen, Nicuesa and his men lived on what food and water they could find in the jungle, which was not much.

Many of the men died of malaria, yellow fever, and exposure to the elements. Later, at a place called Puerto Bello, Nicuesa and his men were attacked by Indians using poison arrows and were forced to move on. Exhausted and low on provisions, legend has it that Nicuesa finally shouted, "*Paremos aqui en el nombre de Dios!*" ("Let us stop here in the name of God"). They did, and from then on, the site was called Nombre de Dios. Only about one hundred men survived from Nicuesa's original expedition of seven hundred.

When reinforcements arrived, a new governor, Martín Fernández de Enciso, was with them. Fernández de Enciso was a poor leader also, but on the advice of a young man named Vasco Núñez de Balboa, he moved the colony west to a site that was safe from attack. Here, at the mouth of what the Indians called the Darién River, the Spaniards set up a new colony, which they named Santa María la Antigua del Darién.

Realizing that Fernández de Enciso was as ill-equipped a leader as Nicuesa, the Spanish colonists unofficially elected Balboa as their governor. Both Nicuesa and Fernández de Enciso were sent back to Spain, and the new colony of Antigua, under the leadership of Balboa, began to thrive. Even those who had remained in Nombre de Dios now abandoned it to strengthen the colony of Antigua. Balboa was not only the leader at Antigua, but he was also the first elected governor of Castillo del Oro, or Panama.

Balboa's Trek to the Ocean

Balboa made further important contributions to the Spanish settlements in Panama. As governor-elect, Balboa proved himself a born leader, even creating peace treaties and pacts with surrounding indigenous tribes. He communicated with them using two Spanish translators who had learned some of the language of the Panamanian Indians.

Comagre, the cacique (chief) of one tribe, learned of Balboa's power and offered him a present of around four thousand ounces of gold to make an alliance. During a peaceful supper between Balboa and Comagre, one of Comagre's sons told Balboa and his men of a giant body of water that lay to the south. This "South Sea," Balboa realized, could very well be a passage to the Orient. European explorers had been looking for a route to the east to open trade between Europe and Asian countries such as India. Comagre's son assured the men that the lands to the south were also rich with gold.

Balboa made it his mission to find the sea. He sent a request to Spain for a thousand more men to make the journey to the sea. He also sent a large quantity of gold as proof of his allegiance to the Spanish court. But the king had already appointed a new governor of Castillo del Oro, Pedro Arias Dávila (often called Pedrarias), a seventy-year-old colonel who was married to one of Queen Isabella's ladies-in-waiting.

Word of Pedrarias's impending arrival prompted Balboa to set out on the expedition to the sea on his own. He took with him 190 Spanish volunteers from Antigua, guided by Comagre's son. They left on September 1, 1513, accompanied by about one thousand Indians, who carried their food and provisions. Balboa defeated more Indian tribes farther south and, either by alliance or through force, made them his guides to the sea.

On the morning of September 25 Balboa climbed the ridge of a mountain from which the Indians told him he would be able to see the body of water on the other side. Upon reaching the top, Balboa became the first European to view what he named the Mar del Sur (the "South Sea"). Four days later Balboa and his men reached the beach and claimed the sea in the name of Spain. Balboa had reached the Pacific Ocean. He returned to Antigua on January 19, 1514, with bundles of plundered gold and the pride of a Spanish hero.

PEDRARIAS

In June 1514 Pedrarias arrived in Antigua and formally became governor of Castillo del Oro.

In 1513 Vasco Núñez de Balboa and his men became the first Europeans to see the Pacific Ocean.

Pedro Arias Dávila, the cruel governor of Castillo del Oro, ordered the slaughter of thousands of Panama's indigenous peoples.

Pedrarias was one of the worst and cruelest administrators in Panama's long history. Within four months after he took over, seven hundred men had died of disease and famine. Almost all of the food the Spanish had brought with them rotted in the tropical climate.

Pedrarias began his reign of cruelty with the Indians. He dissolved many of the treaties Balboa had made with indigenous tribes. Pedrarias sent his men, with their superior weapons—guns, armor, and cannons—along with hunting dogs, to decimate whole tribes, slaughtering men, women and children. Pedrarias was responsible, directly and indirectly, for the practices adopted by the Spanish soldiers and explorers who helped bring about the almost complete destruction of indigenous tribes in Panama by 1530.

Author Christopher Ward describes the effect of Spanish practices on native Panamanian tribes: "The conquest itself was one of the most brutal campaigns witnessed in the Americas. Indians died by the thousands, and those that remained were weakened by the disruption of indigenous society. . . . [And] a major plague killed most survivors of the conquest."[4] Some historians estimate that there were approximately five hundred thousand Indians in over sixty different tribes before the Spanish began these raids, placing the deaths for which Pedrarias was responsible in the hundreds of thousands.

But Pedrarias's cruelty was not limited to the indigenous peoples. As Pedrarias took control, the Spanish court received Balboa's gifts and the news of his discovery of the Pacific Ocean. Author Philip E. Wheaton writes of Spain's reaction to the news:

> Balboa's discovery of the Pacific made the isthmus the highest priority for the Spanish Crown, as it came to be seen as a solution to the problem of finding a way past the American continent and thus "a vehicle of ultramarine communication, toward the supreme goal—the Orient [meaning the trade ports of Asia]."[5]

Balboa's sudden prestige in Spain made Pedrarias extremely jealous, and from then on Pedrarias sought for a way to rid himself and Panama of Balboa's presence. In January 1519 Pedrarias framed Balboa for treason. He had Balboa and some of his officers beheaded in Acla, a town Balboa had helped to found. With Balboa out of the way, Pedrarias was free to control the isthmus as he saw fit. So, on August 15, 1519, Pedrarias founded Panama City, the new capital of Castillo del Oro, on the Pacific coast.

THE TRAIL OF GOLD

The Spanish mined and looted the land and tribes of their gold. As a result, they needed a way to carry their booty from the Pacific side of the isthmus to the Atlantic side, where ships docked to take the gold back to Spain. Mule caravans carrying wealth from Peruvian mines also soon needed a way across to the Atlantic.

The most suitable road was found by Captain Antonio Tello de Guzman, who was under orders from Pedrarias to

THE *CIMMARONES*

Beginning in the sixteenth century, a new group of inhabitants known as the *cimmarones* came to Panama, but not of their own free will. The *cimmarones* were African slaves brought over by the Spanish for the construction of the Camino Real. By 1523 the Spanish government officially endorsed the practice of slavery on the isthmus, and soon boats carrying thousands of African slaves were making regular trips to Spanish colonies.

However, the unique, dense jungle terrain provided the slaves with unequaled opportunities to escape, slipping into the jungle and disappearing within feet of a clearing. Richard F. Nyrop writes in *Panama: A Country Study*, "They became known as *cimmarones*, meaning wild or unruly, because they attacked travelers along the Camino Real."

These *cimmarones* eventually set up whole cities deep within the jungles of Darién. Their capital, Ronconcholon, was a fairly modern village with an estimated seventeen hundred inhabitants. They even had kings, the greatest and most well-known being King Bayano, who fought the Spanish during the 1550s. Because many of these slaves had been transported first into English colonies or had even been raised in the English-controlled West Indies, most of them spoke English. And because they had as much reason as any other group to defy Spanish tyranny on the isthmus, during the sixteenth and seventeenth centuries, several *cimmarones* allied themselves with the English, who called them *Maroons*, acting as guides, informants, and spies for privateers and pirates.

explore the western coast of Castillo del Oro in 1515. Tello de Guzman encountered a Cueva Indian tribe on the west coast. These natives called their village Panama, which, in Cueva, is thought to have meant "abundance of fish" because the natives survived by fishing off the coast.

The natives told Tello de Guzman about a path leading across the isthmus. They had used this path, farther to the west, for hundreds of years, and although it was longer, it was through lower mountains and was thus an easier route than the Spanish had been using. The eastern side of this trail also came out near the abandoned settlement of Nombre de Dios, which still had standing buildings. Thus, the Spanish decided to construct a widened road along this path. The Spanish named the road El Camino Real, "the King's Way."

Slaves played a huge role in constructing the Camino Real. Over four thousand indigenous peoples captured by the Spanish widened the path to accommodate two passing mule carts. It was paved with smooth river stones and clay.

More natives were enslaved along the way, and native villages were used as resting posts for the Spanish engineers. In addition, the Spanish began importing African slaves to supplement the huge task.

The finished road, with a newly constructed bridge across the large Chagres River, brought the abandoned settlement Nombre de Dios back to life. Panama City (named so because it stood on the site of the former Indian village) was at the Pacific end. Peter Martyr, a Spanish theologian and historian of the day, wrote, "The colonists resolved to unite the two settlements by a road. It was therefore laid out at the cost of the king and the colonists, nor was the expense small. Rocks had to be broken up, and wild beasts driven from their lairs."[6] Martyr's assessment did not include the expenses of slave and Indian life, nor did it account for how many natives were driven from their villages.

Panama City became the new capital of Castillo del Oro in 1519. It was made the capital because it was easier to defend than settlements on the Atlantic side. The flow of gold and silver in the form of mule trains was also controlled from this point. From that point on, Panama City was the center of activity on the isthmus and was the most important city in terms of the country's history.

PIRACY IN PANAMA

Spain controlled almost all wealth coming out of Central and South America during the sixteenth century. Because they saw the profits Spain was making, other European countries, particularly England, attempted to cut into Spain's control and establish settlements of their own. But Spanish naval power, military presence, and growing trade in Central and South America and in the Caribbean was so strong that Spain's dominance was almost total. Some of the West Indies were controlled by England, which provided it and other European countries with a base of operations for their only means of retaliation against Spain: a practice known as privateering. Privateers were pirates who were authorized by their home country to attack and pillage ships of enemy countries.

Privateers looted and plundered Spanish ships and settlements and sent part of their booty back to England. In return, England refused to police their activity. The most

famous example of privateering was the English seaman Sir Francis Drake. Between the years of 1572 and 1596, Drake became the most well known English privateer to sail in Caribbean waters.

Even after Drake's death in 1597, piracy continued in the Caribbean Sea, but this did little to slow the overall Spanish export of gold from the Americas. Despite raids by other illustrious pirates such as Sir Walter Raleigh, Spain's precious metal imports tripled during the last half of the sixteenth century. Spanish colonies sprang up around gold and silver mines, mostly in Peru. And for over a century things continued as they were, with Spain shipping gold up to Panama and then out of the Atlantic port of Portobelo, while English privateers sailed the Caribbean waters hoping for a chance to

Panama City became the country's capital in 1519. This seventeenth-century painting depicts ships laden with gold and silver leaving the city's harbor for Spain.

HENRY MORGAN

The Caribbean was home to a specific type of pirate from 1625 to 1698 known as the buccaneer. Buccaneers got their name from the smoke pits called *boucans*, which they used to dry and preserve meats while hiding out on islands in the Caribbean Sea.

The most famous buccaneer was a Welshman named Henry Morgan, born around 1635. When he was still a child, Morgan ran away from his home to become a cabin boy onboard a ship bound for the West Indies. In Barbados, however, Morgan's captain sold him into slavery. A few years later he escaped to Jamaica. He quickly rose to power among the bands of thieves and pirates there.

In 1665 the English government was trying to keep other European countries from profiting from the riches of the Americas, so they commissioned Morgan to create havoc among the competing Dutch and Spanish settlements. He headed for Panama, and in 1668 he sacked Portobelo. By 1670 he had ravaged the Cuban and American coastlines and assembled the largest fleet of buccaneers ever to be put under single control—more than two thousand men in thirty-seven ships.

On January 29, 1671, Morgan and fourteen hundred men raided Panama City, defeating the Spanish and taking with them 175 mules carrying loot. He also took prisoner six hundred men, women, and children, for which he collected ransoms from relatives. Sometime during the occupation of Panama City, which lasted four weeks, someone set fire to the town. The whole city burned to the ground within a few days. Two years later the Spanish rebuilt Panama City, approximately six miles to the west in a more defensible position. For his exploits, the English government knighted Morgan and made him lieutenant governor of Jamaica, where he lived until his death in 1688.

In 1671 the English buccaneer Henry Morgan and his men defeated the Spanish and raided and burned Panama City to the ground.

attack. However, though a successful business for some, privateering had failed in its larger goal of stopping the Spanish from profiting from their hold on Panama and South America.

In the end, the only area that piracy managed to hurt on a large scale was Panama itself, not Spain. Little mining was actually being done in Panama, so Spanish traders simply stopped making the trip up to Panama to export gold because they knew they would just face pirates on the other side. The Spanish began sailing south from Peru, down below the southern tip of South America known as Cape Horn. Although the waters there could be treacherous, it was considered safer than facing privateers. In this way, piracy was partly responsible for Panama's decline in importance to Spain as a transit point.

Panama's decline in importance continued as gold mines in South America dried up. Furthermore, Indian tribes that wore gold and other precious metals began to disappear, killed off or relocated to the remotest areas of Panama. Finally, in 1717, Spain created the royal province of New Granada, in which it lumped present-day Colombia, Ecuador, Panama, and Venezuela into one territory. No longer serving the important port function it once had, Panama became the poorest and least-developed part of New Granada.

PANAMANIAN INDEPENDENCE

It was nearly one hundred years later before Panama would try to break away from Spain. The French Revolution had promoted the ideas of democracy and liberation. The U.S. Declaration of Independence proved that American colonies could secede from European control. And in 1808 Napoléon occupied Spain, weakening its control over its colonies. So at the beginning of the nineteenth century, the province of New Granada successfully seceded from Spanish rule.

Independence was in season; no longer held together by Spanish rule, Venezuela and Ecuador seceded from New Granada in 1829 and 1830, respectively. Panama had tried to secede, too, in 1821. Panamanian officials first publicly declared independence with a document called the *Grito* (literally, the "Shout") *de la Villa de los Santos* on November 10, 1821. But Panama remained a country too weak and too undeveloped to stand alone. As the majority of Panamanians were uneducated and poverty-stricken, Panama simply could not follow the stronger countries into independence. Panama was thus forced to become a province of the nation Gran Colombia, which eventually became Colombia. Colombia divided Panama into two provinces, Panama and Veragua.

The Colombian government took advantage of its rule over smaller Panama. Throughout the nineteenth century, Colombia used many of the same tactics against Panama that Spain had used against its colonies. Colombia taxed the area of Panama without giving Panama's citizens any say in the process. Colombia also falsified elections in order to retain its power. But Panamanians never lost interest in the dream of self-government. From 1830 to 1903, Panama attempted to secede from Colombia five times. Over fifty riots, in fact, caused the United States to intervene thirteen times. Unrest was also caused by the fact that Colombia changed administrations nearly forty times during this same period.

Two particularly serious attempts at Panamanian secession from Colombia occurred mid-century. A man by the name of Thomas Herrera led a movement between 1840 and 1841. What were then known as the provinces of Panama and Veragua declared themselves to be the State of the Isthmus of Panama. They even elected a president and vice president to start a new government. But Colombia threatened military action, and the rebellion was put down. They tried again in 1855, calling themselves the Federal State of Panama, but again met with the same results. As in 1821, extreme illiteracy and poverty in the area resulted in a populace too weak to break free from its oppressive government. Panama remained a province, called a *departmento*, of Colombia until 1903, when the United States took an interest in Panama's future.

THE PANAMA RAILROAD

In the nineteenth century the locomotive replaced the mule train and wagon as the fastest form of freight transport. For this reason, throughout the first half of the century England and France talked with Colombia about building a railroad across the isthmus of Panama. But the huge expense required for such an undertaking always deterred any definite plans. The final decision to build a railroad across the isthmus came from a number of factors that built up throughout the 1840s.

THE SCOTTISH COLONY

William Paterson, a successful businessman and a shrewd financier, was born in Scotland in 1665 and by the end of the century was responsible for gaining support for a Scottish colony in Panama. Scottish financiers raised almost eight hundred thousand British pounds, and on July 17, 1699, around thirteen hundred Scots, mostly men, sailed aboard five ships bound for the jungles of Darién. They planned to call their settlement New Caledonia.

They landed in Darién in November but were ill prepared for the tropical climate and harsh rigors of Panama. The settlement they had planned for was a trading post, not a survival camp. They took with them many trade supplies, such as four thousand wigs, nearly fifteen hundred bonnets, almost a thousand pairs of wool stockings, and twenty tons of brandy. However, they lacked practical goods that would have helped them survive Panama's heat and rainy season.

Several other factors doomed the project to failure. The Spanish opposed the Scottish attempt and repeatedly attacked the newly constructed Scottish fort. But disease, not the Spanish, was the worst killer of Scottish settlers. What is presumed to have been yellow fever and malaria killed them off a hundred at a time. By the summer of 1700 about 750 of the men who made the original journey were dead either from disease or by the hands of the Spanish. And although a ship of around 1,300 more men arrived that same year, the same fate befell them. Within another year, 940 of these men were dead. By 1702 the project was abandoned, with nearly everyone dead or scattered. Paterson made his way to New York and eventually back to Scotland, a broken man. He was not the first to be defeated by the isthmus, and he was definitely not the last.

It all began when American settlers on the eastern seaboard became bound for California. They found that going through Panama was a good way to travel west. Ships left from eastern seaports like New York and carried settlers down the eastern coast, landing in Panama. These settlers then crossed the isthmus on foot and caught a boat on the other side that took them up to the western coast of the United States. The settlers found that this route was faster and less dangerous than the trek west across the U.S. mainland. During the 1840s the U.S. Postal Service secured rights to pass mail through Panama from east to west and vice versa using the same route as the settlers.

Finally, the discovery of gold on January 24, 1848, in California inspired demand for a fast way across Panama.

Prospective gold miners—called "forty-niners" for the year the gold rush occurred—not only wanted to get to the west coast but also get there quickly. Like the settlers, forty-niners learned that the Panama route was the quickest and safest. But they also found that the slowest and most laborious part of the trip was walking on foot across the isthmus. The gold rush also escalated the need for a train across the isthmus to carry mail because correspondence increased between people who had moved to California and the families they had left behind. Finally, on April 15, 1850, the U.S.-owned Panama Railroad Company signed a contract with the government of Colombia to build a railroad across the isthmus.

International influence in the country began as laborers from various countries flowed in to work on the railroad. Workers from the West Indies, England, Ireland, Germany,

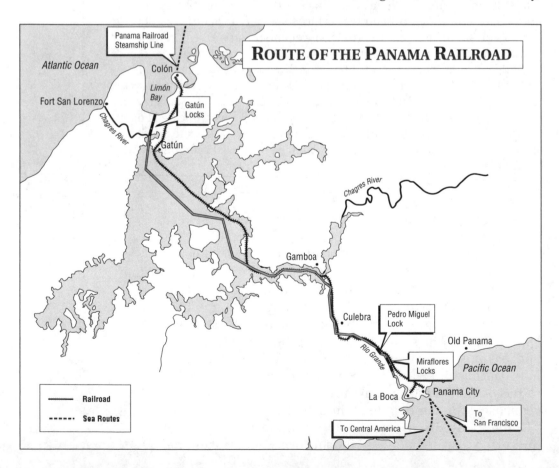

ROUTE OF THE PANAMA RAILROAD

and China, among other countries, were all represented. Unfortunately, death and disease plagued the operation from the start. Dysentery, cholera, yellow fever, malaria, smallpox, and a host of other problems, including suicide and on-the-job accidents, killed thousands of workers between 1850 and 1855, when the railroad opened. Some estimates put the death toll at six thousand, but others set it as high as ten thousand or more. Of all the workers, West Indian blacks may have fared best: They were accustomed to the heat, and similar strains of diseases in the West Indies had given them some immunity to diseases like malaria and yellow fever.

The Panama Railroad was finally opened on January 27, 1855, having cost nearly $7.5 million. It spanned forty-seven miles and 304 waterways, becoming the first intercontinental railroad in the world, eventually carrying up to fifteen hundred passengers per day. A trip from Panama City to Colón on the Atlantic side took over three hours and cost twenty-five dollars, which was a steep price at the time. Massive amounts of people and goods began crisscrossing the isthmus in transport and trade. Panama was reinvigorated as an international passageway. And although the railroad had brought great fame to the region, it was only a matter of time before an even more impressive project was undertaken on the isthmus.

3

THE AGE OF INDUSTRY, INDEPENDENCE, AND POLITICS

For Panama, the nineteenth and twentieth centuries were some of the most active two hundred years a country has ever seen. Panama's landscape, politics, and culture changed several times throughout this period, and much of what occurred still bears overwhelming relevance to life in Panama today.

THE FRENCH CANAL PROJECT

Today the Panama Canal is the most important piece of property in Panama, but originally, no Panamanians had anything to do with the decision to build a canal through the region. Wealthy businessmen from around the world recognized the potential worth of creating a canal through Panama. Ships going from the Pacific to the Atlantic Ocean, and vice versa, would be able to pass through Panama with their goods without unloading onto a train. The land around the canal would become a natural center of trade. And the tolls that ships would pay to pass through the canal would bring in a great deal of money.

A minor French diplomat named Ferdinand de Lesseps was the first to see the full potential of a canal in Panama. Lesseps had been the leader of the Suez Canal project in Egypt, which opened on November 17, 1869. The Suez Canal was important because it linked the Mediterranean Sea and the Red Sea, eliminating the need for ships to sail around the southern tip of Africa. Lesseps felt that the same thing could be done for the Americas. By cutting a waterway through Panama, ships would no longer be forced to sail around the southern tip of South America to pass from the Atlantic to the Pacific Ocean. So, Lesseps used his success with the Suez Canal to gather support for a canal in Panama.

In 1879 he led talks at the International Congress for Studies of the Interoceanic Canal in which twenty-two countries met to express their interest in a canal through Panama. Among countries represented were the United States, Colombia, China, Belgium, Great Britain, Italy, Hawaii (still its own nation), and France. Despite proposals for other routes, it was decided that the canal would cut through the center of the isthmus at one of the thinnest spots of land between the seas—about forty miles. The congress acted quickly, and by 1880 the first members of the newly formed Universal Company of the Interoceanic Canal arrived in Panama. By January 1881 the first group of French engineers arrived to begin construction on the canal.

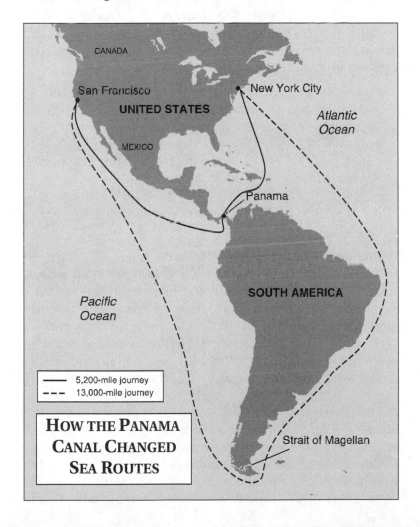

HOW THE PANAMA
CANAL CHANGED
SEA ROUTES

DISEASE

The canal project was immediately befallen by disease—one of the biggest killers of men in Panama. The two most deadly diseases were yellow fever and malaria. Over time, malaria claimed the most lives of men constructing the canal, but men feared yellow fever more because it hit in waves, spreading quickly and killing in the most awful fashion. Some of its symptoms were backache, vomiting, high fever, shock, bleeding, and liver failure. Liver failure caused jaundice, which caused the skin and whites of the eyes to turn yellow. Thus, the disease got its name from the appearance of its victims.

In June 1881 the first canal employee died from yellow fever. Both malaria and yellow fever were spread by mosquitoes, but doctors did not yet understand this. David McCullough, in *The Path Between the Seas*, writes about the medical misconceptions:

> Yellow fever . . . was believed to be airborne, but filth was supposedly its source—sewage, the putrefying carcasses of dead animals, all the distasteful human and animal waste to be found in the streets of Colon or Panama City. The greatest source of contamination supposedly was the patient himself, and to touch his clothing, his soiled bedding, anything he had come in contact with, [was believed to mean] almost certain death.[7]

Estimates on the number of deaths ranged from two to three out of every four French workers to arrive in Panama. It was also estimated that one out of every three workers, French or otherwise, was sick during the French construction effort; this meant that by 1884, at any given time about six thousand workers out of nineteen thousand were sick. The most accepted estimate is that twenty-two thousand people died during the nearly decade-long French canal project.

AN EXPENSIVE UNDERTAKING

Sickness was not the only problem that plagued the French effort. The French had seriously underestimated the cost of building what Lesseps insisted must be a sea-level canal, which essentially meant digging a flat trench from ocean to ocean. But there were mountains and high land to dig

THE WATERMELON RIOT

U.S. involvement in Panama has always been a source of resentment and turmoil. One of the first incidents of violent anti-American sentiment occurred after the Panama Railroad's completion in 1855, which caused nearly two thousand Panamanian workers once employed in its construction to be out of work. This unemployment caused a wave of poverty throughout Colón and Panama City, resulting in resentment among poor Panamanians.

This resentment erupted on April 15, 1856, when a U.S. mail steamship arrived in Colón carrying a thousand passengers. An American passenger, Jack Oliver, had been drinking with friends and became rude and loud on the train to Panama City. Once there, Oliver stole a slice of watermelon from a black peddler and refused to pay him the ten cents he owed. The peddler grew enraged and pulled out a knife. Oliver drew a pistol. Another poor Panamanian nearby attempted to wrestle the gun away; in the chaos, a bystander was shot and wounded. This caused the surrounding Panamanian crowd to erupt into an anti-American mob. The mob began looting Americans' hotel rooms, shops, and the railroad. More than three thousand Americans were in Panama City, and many were beaten, robbed, and even murdered.

A large group of Americans took refuge in the train depot. Police officers now began making their way toward the depot, presumably to disperse the attacking mob. But Americans began firing guns from inside the depot and accidentally shot and killed one of the police officers. The police then joined the mob and attacked the depot. When the mob broke down the door, the depot watchman fired an antique Spanish cannon, killing one of the attackers and wounding several others. But the mob poured in and killed the agent and other Americans hiding in the room. The Americans then fired from the second floor down the stairs at the mob, holding them off until finally a train carrying a Panamanian railroad guard arrived and dispersed the crowd, thus ending one of the bloodiest and earliest episodes of anti-Americanism in Panama.

through to get down to sea level. The highest was a place called Culebra, where most of the digging on the canal eventually took place.

An alternative plan would have been to build a lock canal, which Lesseps rejected. Locks are like giant tubs that are connected like stairs. A boat moves into the lowest tub. The tub fills with water to raise the boat to the level of the next tub. The boat moves into the next tub, a door is shut, and the process is repeated in the second lock. This can be done to raise and lower boats over land that is too high to be cut down to sea level.

Laborers use shovels and railcars to clear dirt for the sea-level canal envisioned by French diplomat Ferdinand de Lesseps.

The real failure of the French company was failing to understand that Panama was a very different place than the dry desert of Suez, Egypt. Suez had been a sea-level canal. Thus, Lesseps insisted that this was the best way to go about constructing a canal in Panama. But, Panama's terrain was too hilly. The jungles, disease, and muddy earth all kept the idea of a sea-level canal from working. Funding sputtered, and the company developed serious money problems. The company failed and officially went out of business on February 4, 1889. Machinery brought to Panama from France was preserved as Lesseps tried to restart the company with more capital, but a second company failed as well.

Ferdinand de Lesseps died on December 7, 1894, having never realized his dream of creating a waterway through the Americas. It is estimated that his project, lasting over a decade, cost the company and French shareholders more than $287 million, the largest sum ever expended on any single nonwar effort to that date.

GORGAS AND THE MOSQUITO

One of the most important men in the effort to build the Panama Canal was William Crawford Gorgas. Born in 1854 in Mobile, Alabama, he joined the army in 1880. At Fort Brown, Texas, he was stricken with yellow fever. He recovered and then had an immunity to the disease, a trait that would guide his career in the years to come.

In 1898 Gorgas was sent to Havana, Cuba, where an epidemic of yellow fever was raging. A common house mosquito, *Stegomyia fasciata*, was the carrier of yellow fever; each time it bit a human, it would pass along the disease. In Cuba, Gorgas set out on a campaign to eradicate the *Stegomyia* mosquito. In 1901, within eight months of the mosquito campaign's beginning, yellow fever was gone in Havana.

In 1904 Gorgas was sent to Panama to achieve the same thing. Panama's climate and terrain combined to create a mosquito paradise. The temperature barely changes year-round, so mosquitoes were always breeding. Furthermore, pockets of standing water—where mosquitoes lay their eggs—were everywhere, from footprints in muddy roads to small bowls of water placed beneath the legs of hospital beds to keep ants away.

Most of Gorgas's work, and the work of his team in the years to come, involved these sources of standing water. He either got rid of the water altogether or sprayed a thin layer of kerosene on the water, which floated on the top and killed mosquitoes. Gorgas worked in Panama during the entire building of the Panama Canal. He began his campaign in 1905, and within a year and a half he had almost rid the canal's populace of yellow fever. Had he not done this, it is estimated that around three to four thousand people would have died every year from the disease, about the same toll that resulted in the French catastrophe.

By controlling the mosquito population in Panama, William Crawford Gorgas helped contain the spread of yellow fever.

DECLARING INDEPENDENCE

The United States took over where the French had failed. Phillipe Bunau-Varilla, a French officer in the failed French Canal Company, convinced the United States to invest in a new canal project and buy the land, equipment, and rights for $40 million. The Hay-Herrera Treaty was signed on January 22, 1903, with Colombia. The treaty stated that the United States would take over all the rights, privileges, properties, and concessions previously granted to the French company. For one hundred years, the United States would lease a six-mile-wide strip stretching from Colón to Panama City. The United States would pay Colombia $10 million and then an annual rent of $250,000, beginning nine years later. The United States would have control over all the ports, the canal, the railroad, and its own courts within this area.

However, the Colombian government was not satisfied with the agreed-upon amount and did not ratify the treaty. But the United States was unwilling to enter into lengthy negotiations with Colombia, so it used Panamanian unrest to its advantage. At the urging of Bunau-Varilla, Panamanian officials declared their independence from Colombia on November 3, 1903, with the promise of U.S. support. President Theodore Roosevelt recognized the new Panamanian government three days later. Panama's first leaders were predominantly prominent, wealthy, white members of powerful families on the Panamanian isthmus; their descendants ruled Panama until 1968.

Phillipe Bunau-Varilla, acting as the Panamanian representative to the United States, signed the Hay–Bunau-Varilla Treaty with John Hay, the U.S. secretary of state, without a single member of the newly formed Panamanian government present. This transferred the concessions of the Hay-Herran Treaty from Colombia to Panama. The Panamanian officials protested, but fearing the United States would pull out completely, leaving them open to Colombian retaliation over their secession, they ratified the treaty on December 2. Because of the treaty, the Republic of Panama came under the protection of the United States on February 23, 1904. The treaty also gave the United States the power to intervene in Panama's domestic affairs if the canal was threatened.

THE PANAMA CANAL

The Panama Canal was a gigantic architectural undertaking unlike any other in history. David McCullough explains the magnitude of the Panama Canal project:

> Dollar expenditures since 1904 totaled $352,000,000 ... so much more than the cost of anything ever before built by the United States government. Taken together, the French and American expenditures came to about $639,000,000.... The total price in human life may have been as high as twenty-five thousand, or five hundred lives for every mile of the canal. The total excavation accomplished ... [was] 262,000,000 cubic yards [of earth] using more than 61,000,000 pounds of dynamite, a greater amount of explosive energy than had been expended in all the nation's wars until that time.[8]

The amount of earth moved was equal to a city block almost twenty miles high, and though the accomplishment was great, it had not come easily or quickly. The United States officially took over the Panama Canal project on May 4, 1904. By December of the following year, over twenty-six hundred men were at work digging on what became known as the Culebra Cut, and later as Gaillard Cut, which alone accounted for over $90 million of the total project cost. This eight-mile-long excavation, which was forty-five feet deep over the Culebra Mountains, used one hundred ninety-five-ton steam shovels to dig more than thirty million cubic feet of earth per day.

In 1906 the United States, realizing the ridiculousness of attempting to dig through the mountains of Panama, opted to construct a lock canal instead of a sea-level one. But the locks themselves were a huge engineering feat. Crushed rock from Culebra Cut was used to make the three sets of locks, known as Gatún on the Atlantic side and Pedro Miguel and Miraflores on the Pacific. The locks took four years to build. Construction began on the first lock, at Gatún, on August 24, 1909, by pouring concrete from giant buckets overhead. Its walls were one-thousand-feet long and were as tall as a six-story building. According to McCullough, "A single lock if stood on end would have been the tallest structure in the world, taller even than the Eiffel Tower."[9] In all, more than 2 million cubic yards of concrete were poured. After nearly

The enormous gates of a lock at Gatún are under construction. The intricate lock system of the Panama Canal remains an engineering marvel.

thirty-four years of construction, the Panama Canal was opened to its first seafaring vessel, the *Ancon*, on August 15, 1914, which passed through without a hitch.

The official Web site of the Panama Canal explains its importance today:

> Some 13 to 14 thousand vessels use the Canal every year. In fact, commercial transportation activities through the Canal represent approximately 5% of the world trade. The Canal has a work force of approximately 9 thousand employees and operates 24 hours a day, 365

days a year, providing transit service to vessels of all nations without discrimination.[10]

The opening of the canal, however, was overshadowed by the fact that German troops were headed for Paris, signaling the beginning of World War I.

PANAMANIAN RESENTMENT

From the time of its independence in 1903 through the next fifty years, the central source of debate for Panama's government was its relationship with the United States. In the beginning, the country was controlled by an oligarchy, a government made up of a few powerful and wealthy families. This oligarchy was often unsympathetic to the needs of its poor citizens. The United States had helped to put these families in power, which meant that, almost immediately, poor and working-class Panamanians resented the United States as an overbearing force in the development of their country.

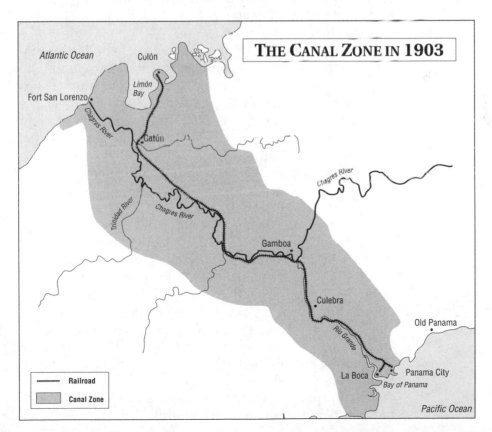

However, Panamanian independence relied on the protection of the United States. In the role of protector, the United States was permitted the right to intercede in Panama's domestic affairs if they threatened the safety of the U.S. Canal Zone. For instance, the United States would not intervene in any revolts within Panama over control of its own government unless that revolt threatened the canal or the U.S. citizens living in the Canal Zone.

The Canal Zone, however, was more than just a strip of land; it was a moneymaking area of commerce, and so long as the United States controlled all of it, little of the money from its operation leaked into Panama. And then, even when it did, it was the oligarchy that stood to make the money. The United States also implemented its own regulations, customs, and postal service in the zone, a move the Panamanian government opposed because it further funneled profits from the Canal Zone to the United States. The point of U.S. sovereignty (authority to govern) and its actual boundaries remained a topic of heated debate throughout the U.S. occupation of the Canal Zone.

Finally, in 1932 unrest among the people of Panama resulted in the election of a nonoligarchy president, Harmodio Arias. He obtained the presidency by using a political platform that attacked the old political system of the wealthy families for ignoring the problem of Panamanian poverty. Thus, Arias was the first president to institute governmental relief efforts. His brother, Arnulfo, followed in his footsteps and became one of the people's strongest leaders.

THE RISE OF THE MILITARY

Arnulfo Arias used the popular anti-American sentiment as the foundation of his platform. He helped to institute laws that moved U.S. troops off bases not within the Canal Zone. As a result, military leaders like José Antonio Remon, who opposed the Arias brothers, gained American support. Remon became the Commander of the National Police, Panama's military force. Remon gained power by helping the United States remove Arnulfo Arias from office. Because of U.S backing and his increasing power over the government, Remon was elected president in 1952. Because he was head of both the military and the civilian government, Panama fell more and more under military control.

HARMODIO AND ARNULFO ARIAS

Arias relied heavily on fanning anti-American sentiment among middle-class Panamanians to support his campaign for president. Arias and his supporters believed that U.S. power had made it possible for corrupt, wealthy families to stay in power in the Panamanian government. As part of his attempted reformation of the country, Arias founded the University of Panama, which helped bring higher education to the middle classes. Even to-day, the school reflects the middle-class political view against oligarchy and U.S. power over Panama.

There was much debate over the rights of the United States in Panama. By 1939 Harmodio had pushed the United States into agreeing to a treaty that helped Panamanian merchants compete with U.S. merchants in the Panama Canal Zone. By 1940 unrest among the middle classes was high, and Harmodio's brother, Arnulfo, was elected under an anti-American, national-ist platform. The views of this platform, however, bordered on racism and fascism (a rigid political regime led by a dictator who employs strict social and economic regimentation). Arnulfo even implemented laws designed to rid the country of non-Hispanic, non-Spanish-speaking parts of the popula-tion. He tried to deport West Indian (Antillean) blacks, and he expressed ap-proval of the tactics of Nazi Germany and Fascist Italy, whose leaders were gaining power in Europe. These views made him highly unpopular with the American government. He was ousted by the National Police, with backing from the United States, in 1941.

Over the course of his political career, Arnulfo was elected three times: in 1940, 1949, and 1968. He was never allowed to retain his office. He was re-moved every time by military means. It is widely believed that he was elected in 1964 and 1984, but the fraudulent elections were rigged against him. Despite his racism, many of Arnulfo's tactics brought about change. By 1948 nationalis-tic sentiment among the working class had helped to bring about treaties with the United States that moved unwanted U.S. troops off bases other than those within the Canal Zone.

The increasing military control over the country only es-calated tension between the government's military and the people. By 1958 tensions were so high that students of the University of Panama, a major source of political unrest and anti-American activity, erupted in a riot in which nine were killed when military units attempted to control them.

The most symbolic clash between the anti-American Panamanians and the military came in 1964 during what be-came known as the Flag Riots. An agreement had been reached in 1963 between the United States and Panama that wherever U.S. flags were flown, so too would be flown the Panamanian flag. This agreement was meant to be a symbolic gesture of America's acknowledgment of Panama's rights in the Canal Zone.

But in 1964 U.S. students at Balboa High School in the Canal Zone flew only the American flag in front of the building for two days. On January 9, 1964, almost two hundred Panamanian students arrived to demand the hoisting of their flag. When the Panamanian flag was torn during the ensuing struggle, rioting erupted and lasted for three days, spilling to other parts of the Canal Zone and arousing thousands of Panamanians, who inflicted considerable damage on American properties. At these Flag Riots, at least twenty-three people were killed, four hundred were wounded, and almost five hundred were arrested.

Clashes between the military and citizens increased, and by 1968 Panama was in a state of turmoil. Arnulfo Arias recaptured the presidency by winning another election. But by now the military had gained even more power over the country. The military, now called the National Guard, again removed Arias because he had attempted to have the highest-ranking military officers removed. Arias had only been in office ten days. José Maria Pinilla, one of the officers whom Arias had attempted to get rid of, assumed the temporary role of president, promising to again hold free elections the next year. But such a promise was not fulfilled.

Omar Torrijos Herrera

The rise in military power over the government meant that democracy in Panama was breaking down, making conditions right for the rise of a dictator. The commander of the National Guard, General Omar Torrijos Herrera, quickly assumed almost complete control over the National Guard in 1968.

Torrijos Herrera rallied support for his regime with the peoples' two common threads of hatred: the oligarchy and the American domination. This secured him popularity among the tumultuous student groups at the University of Panama. Land reforms and governmental land distribution plans made him popular with small farmers. Loyalty was rewarded in the form of government jobs; disloyalty was met with exile and execution. Torrijos Herrera even pleased wealthy Panamanian businessmen by promising to gain Panamanian sovereignty over the Panama Canal.

In 1972 Torrijos Herrera supported the formation of the 505-member National Assembly of Municipal Representatives that voted to confirm his role as the leader of Panama. The assembly ratified the first of Panama's new constitutions, greatly enhancing Torrijos Herrera's power. Tom Barry and the authors of *Inside Panama* describe this move:

> The 1972 Political Constitution gave the military enough power to shape all State institutions. The National Guard, according to the constitution, became the

General Omar Torrijos Herrera wielded enormous political power in Panama. He signed a treaty with the United States in 1977 giving Panama authority over the Canal Zone.

fourth state power along with the executive, legislative and judicial branches. Torrijos, the National Guard's Commander-in-Chief, was authorized by the constitution to serve as Head of Government for six years.[11]

Torrijos Herrera fulfilled his promise of gaining Panamanian sovereignty over the Canal Zone. In 1977 he signed a treaty with U.S. president Jimmy Carter that ceded the canal to Panama by the end of 1999. Though the change of sovereignty over the canal was years away, the treaty represented a promise by the U.S. to fully withdraw from Panama in the future. Panama's full independence was on the visible horizon.

Despite this success, Torrijos Herrera realized that in order to support the needs of Panamanians, the country had to return to a democracy. Shortly after the signing of the treaty, Torrijos Herrera announced his plans to democratize Panama and reduce the power of the National Guard, turning the government over to a civilian presidency. Plans for the first fully democratic election were set for 1984. Torrijos Herrera promised to see Panama through to a fully functional democracy. But Torrijos Herrera's program for democratization was cut short when he was killed in a mysterious plane crash on July 31, 1981.

MANUEL NORIEGA

The death of Torrijos Herrera ensured the continuation of military control over Panama. The rise of Panama's next dictator came about through the 1984 presidential election. A general in the National Guard, now called the Panama Defense Forces (PDF), Manuel Antonio Noriega rose to the position of commander in chief just before the 1984 elections were held. Technically, whoever would become president would be in command of the PDF, but Noriega realized he now occupied the real position of power.

Noriega backed a politician named Ardito Barletta, a former economist and minister of planning whom Noriega hoped to control. Barletta's opponent was none other than Arnulfo Arias. A key component in Arias's platform was reduction of military spending, which did not appeal to the power-hungry Noriega. Thus, it is believed that in 1984 Noriega rigged the presidential elections, placing his own candidate, Barletta, in the presidency. In 1985, however, when

Barletta failed to obey Noriega's orders, Noriega had him removed, replacing him with an even weaker vice president. Noriega was soon abusing his privileges as the most powerful man in Panama to profit from major drug trafficking.

The United States saw that Noriega's abuse of power was getting out of control and decided to support efforts to have him removed. The United States therefore encouraged Panamanian coup attempts. The first coup failed in March 1988. The United States then announced sanctions against Panama in 1988. Noriega's control over the nation continued, however, and in 1989 the Legislative Assembly (formerly the National Assembly) voted him the head of government with unlimited powers. In October 1989 a second failed coup attempt took place in which seventy-seven men were killed.

A U.S. soldier patrols a street in front of buildings destroyed during the 1989 U.S. invasion of Panama to oust Manuel Noriega from power.

THE U.S. INVASION AND DEMOCRACY FOR PANAMA

With no further options, the United States made the decision to forcefully remove Noriega from power and restore
democracy to Panama. In December 1989 the United States
invaded Panama with twenty-six thousand troops in what
was named Operation Just Cause. The United States cited
several reasons for the invasion: the protection of American
lives, the defense of democracy, the protection of the canal,
and the need to stop Noriega's drug ring in Panama.

Noriega surrendered to U.S. forces in January 1990 and
was later taken back to the United States by agents of the U.S.
Drug Enforcement Administration to stand trial for his
crimes. He was convicted on drug trafficking charges in
Miami, Florida, and was sentenced to prison. Following
Noriega's capture, the United States installed as president
Guillermo Endara Galimany, a candidate from the 1989 elec-
tion that had been annulled for reasons of fraud.

Controversy still revolves around the United States invasion of Panama. Although the United States only recognized
five hundred Panamanians killed in the invasion, international estimates consider the number somewhere between
three thousand and four thousand, many of them innocent
civilians. The U.S. invasion was condemned by the United
Nations' (UN) General Assembly by a vote of seventy-five to
twenty and was considered a violation of the UN Charter and
international law. Some critics argued that the United States
had known about Noriega's drug trafficking for years, but
only now feared they may not be able to control his activity.

In 1994, in the first fully democratic election since 1948,
Ernesto Perez Balladares, a Panamanian businessman, won
the presidency. In 1997, though much anti-American senti-
ment still lingered, he agreed that a small number of U.S.
troops would be allowed to maintain minimal operations in
Panama. In the 1999 elections Mireya Moscoso, the widow of
Arnulfo Arias, was elected president under the Arnulfista
Party. On December 31 she saw her husband's dream of at-
taining Panamanian sovereignty over the canal come true.
Finally, Panama was truly independent.

PRESENT-DAY PANAMA

4

As of July 2003, Panama had a population of 2,960,784 people. That is roughly one one-hundredth the size of the United States in population, or about the same number of people who live in Iowa. But this tiny country has a culture, government, economy, and diversity of populace every bit as complex and layered as any of the world's largest countries. Present-day Panama is a thriving community of varied nationalities and ethnic groups. It is teeming with a wide array of domestic industry supplemented by international trade and regulated by a government growing in strength and capability.

THE GOVERNMENT

Panama's full name is the Republic of Panama. Its government is known as a constitutional democracy, which is also the governmental system used by the United States, Japan, Germany, and several other countries. In fact, Panama's constitution is based on that of the United States. The authority of the government is granted by the consent of the people, usually through regular and free elections. Panama's first democratic constitution was drawn up on October 11, 1972. Since then, it has gone through three major reforms, in 1978, 1983, and most recently in 1994.

Panama's federal government is divided into three branches: the executive, the legislative, and the judicial. The executive branch consists of a president, two vice presidents, and a cabinet, which includes ministers to several departments. There are also such specialized departments as the Ministry of Women, Youth, Family, and Childhood and the Ministry of Canal Affairs. All of these positions are elected by free, secret vote every five years. Representatives of the seventy-one-member single-house legislature are also elected every five years. The judicial branch is divided into three parts—three courts of appeal, five superior courts, and the highest court in the country, the Supreme Court of Justice, whose nine members are appointed and serve a term of ten years.

All voting and voter registration, as well as political activity by all political parties, is monitored by an autonomous group known as the Electoral Tribunal. By law, everyone over the age of eighteen is required to vote, though there is as yet no penalty in place for not doing so.

This federal government, which only fully materialized in the 1990s, has made leaps and bounds toward becoming a fair and stable leadership for its people. Since Manuel Noriega's military was ousted, there has been far less military interference and violence against political leaders. Also, as cities grow and roadways improve, more people find it easier to get to the polls on election day, ensuring that more of the general population's interests are represented when choosing a leader.

EDUCATION

Improved government has in turn improved Panama's education system. The first six years of school are compulsory in Panama. More than 350,000 students are enrolled in grades one through six, and 207,000 are enrolled in grades six through twelve. Panama has a high literacy rate: 93 percent of Panamanians can read. There are fourteen schools of higher education, including the Catholic university Santa María la Antigua, the Technological University, and the largest, the University of Panama. More than 65,000 students attend these universities.

Many of Panama's rural areas are still very poor, which means that many of the children attending school in these areas do not have the same educational opportunities as children in more developed and urban areas. To remedy this, Panama's Ministry of Education has taken out international loans to build new school buildings and renovate nearly three hundred old ones. The ministry also purchased nearly thirty-seven thousand bilingual textbooks in 2000 to help educate children from native Indian tribes. These children often do not speak Spanish, and so new bilingual textbooks present information in both Spanish and their native languages.

Children in many of Panama's rural areas leave school after the elementary levels in order to help on farms, raise cattle, or simply attain jobs doing manual labor. Some rural areas simply have no secondary education available. For this

reason, the Ministry of Education has also established a system of "distance learning" for students from the seventh through ninth grades called *telesecundaria* by using newly built centers and educational materials.

Two Panamanian children in a small village walk to school together. The Panamanian government provides a basic education to all its citizens.

WOMEN

Educational advancements are notably paying off in many ways for the women of Panama. Until recently most women were destined to become housewives rather than career women. Today, however, women make up more than 52 percent of college enrollments. And this education is starting to lead to important societal positions. In government, for example, Mireya Moscoso became Panama's first female president in 1999. Although women hold only seven of the seventy-one seats in the Legislative Assembly, they have succeeded more notably in other areas. Three different women held the position of vice president of the Legislative Assembly from 1999 to 2002, each serving one-year terms. Also in 2002, one of the two women on the Supreme Court held the position of chief justice. In addition, three women hold cabinet seats.

However, women in Panama still face discrimination. Women did not gain the same voting rights as men until 1946. Discrepancies in the laws remained long after, though. Until late into the twentieth century, grounds for divorce between a married couple were a long-term and permanent affair on the part of the husband or a one-time affair on the part of the wife. Mistresses for married husbands were, until recently, an accepted practice by a large part of Panamanian society.

Discriminatory practices for jobs are not much different. Many lower-class families see the men go off to work raising crops or livestock while the women rear the children, leaving them with few other opportunities. Even for women who can enter the workforce, there are other barriers. Companies do not want to pay extra medical costs, so many force women to take pregnancy tests before they are hired and fire women if they become pregnant. Also, in order to avoid paying severance pay to women, many of these companies force female employees to sign only three-month-long contracts, meaning they can be let go after this time at no charge to the employer. Women own or manage less than 10 percent of businesses in Panama today.

Many women find employment doing domestic jobs like cleaning houses, but most of this kind of work is not regulated by the government, so women can end up working overly long days with no breaks. There is also

Elected in 1999, Mireya Moscoso is Panama's first female president.

another pitfall for these women, which Tom Barry and the authors of *Inside Panama* explain: "Another common source of employment for working-class women is the export-oriented industrial sector. Laboring under sweatshop conditions, thousands of Panamanian women assemble clothes for export for . . . textile companies."[12] To combat these kinds of business practices, several women's associations have been formed, among them, the Women's National Coordination, the National Forum for Women and Development, and the Women's Department of the Ministry of Labor.

Despite these barriers, even women without higher educations have still made advances. In 1999, in the rural farming community of Canglon just outside Darién National Park, thirteen women started the Association of the Women

THE *POLLERA*

The *pollera* is Panama's official national dress for women, which means that it can be seen at carnivals, celebrations, and gatherings all across the country and is a symbol of Panamanian nationality. *Pollera* literally means "full skirt with many gathers," though the word has come to pertain to the entire dress.

Many theories exist about the origins of the *pollera*. Some believe it was originally the dress of servants, particularly nursemaids during the days of the Spanish colonies. Still others believe that it comes from Spanish high society dresses of the seventeenth century. Yet another theory is that it was originally a kind of dress worn by black slaves.

There are three types of *pollera*: the formal *pollera*, the wedding *pollera*, and the *pollera montuna*. The first, the formal *pollera*, is the dress most people associate with Panama and is what most people think of when they hear the word. Made for footivilies, it is usually a white dress embroidered with vibrantly colored stitching in combinations of designs, traditionally of flowers or birds. The formal *pollera* is by far the most intricate, and strict guidelines often accompany its wearing. The hair must be worn in two tightly pulled braids and adorned with tiny gold ornaments toward the back of the head. Several gold chains are worn around the neck and often consist of pearl and gold rosaries. The skirt must reach the ankles and be tied at the waist with four ribbons, two crossing in front and two in the back. A wedding *pollera* is similar to the formal *pollera* except that the stitching and ornamentation is usually white as well. A *pollera montuna*, on the other hand, is a simple affair—a very colorful skirt made from calico fabric that is worn with a blouse with one ruffle.

of Canglon. These women, who each had between five and seven children, were relying on their husbands, who usually only made a few dollars a day, to provide for their families. The women formed a cooperative group, growing, selling, and experimenting with methods of sustaining crops of yucca, plantains, and aloe vera. This new income helped them play a greater role in securing their families' welfares. Though several problems still face women in Panama, the women of Canglon represent part of a steadily increasing cultural change in the country, a change that has seen women in all walks of life more and more empowered.

Panamanian Rod Carew hits the ball in play as a California Angel. Carew was one of baseball's greatest players.

SPORTS

Women and men alike share a love of sports in Panama. Panama's national sport is baseball, which is taken very seriously. Perhaps Panama's greatest baseball player is the great batter Rod Carew, who played for the Minnesota Twins and the California Angels over a period of fifteen seasons, finishing with a .332 career batting average. He won the American League's batting title six times throughout his career, at one point doing it four years in a row from 1972 to 1975.

But baseball is not the only sport in Panama. Unlike many other popular sports that have come from all over the world, one sport originated in Panama. The sport is *cayuco* racing. In Panama, the word *cayuco* refers to a dugout canoe carved from a single tree. In a yearly event, called the Ocean-to-Ocean Cayuco Race, which is sponsored by the Balboa Paddle Club, competitors of all ages, male and female, compete by paddling their *cayucos* nearly fifty miles through the Panama Canal during a three-day period.

The race began in 1954 by a

ROBERTO DURAN

A popular sport in Panama is boxing. Perhaps the best-known sports hero in Panama is a boxer named Roberto Duran. Duran was born on June 16, 1951. He began boxing when he was a young teenager. Duran became known as *Manos de Piedra*, which means "Hands of Stone," a name his many opponents had to agree with.

Duran did well as an amateur, and in 1967 he decided to turn professional at the age of sixteen. Duran drew attention to himself by winning a streak of twenty-one fights without a formal manager. Then a wealthy businessman bought his contract for three hundred dollars and gave Duran his own trainers. On June 26, 1972, Duran won the World Boxing Association Lightweight Championship. In 1980, in fifteen rounds, he won the World Boxing Council Welterweight Championship from the great American boxer Sugar Ray Leonard, handing Leonard one of only three losses in his career. In 1983 Duran won the WBA Junior Middleweight Championship. Duran continued to box, and as late as June 2000, at nearly fifty years old, he won the National Boxing Association Middleweight Championship. Roberto Duran finally retired in 2002 after almost thirty-five years of boxing. He remains one of only four men in boxing history to hold four different world titles.

troop leader for Boy Scouts of America. He wanted the boys in his troop to meet and learn about a native community of Choco Indians on the Chagres River. The Indians showed the boys how to steer the *cayucos*, which were and still are a main source of transportation for many native tribes all over Panama. The race began as a friendly competition between the boys to test the skills they had learned from the Indians. Soon, however, a formal competition was organized to test these skills, and a race was set to traverse the length of the Panama Canal.

The race celebrated its fiftieth anniversary in 2003, and since its inception it has seen many changes. Competing teams still usually get their boats from Choco Indian craftsmen, but now *cayuco* racers try to shape the outside of the rough wood canoe into a more aerodynamic form. Then they paint it, usually in bright colors, to display their team name. There are now two classes of competitors for the *cayuco* race: youth, which includes ages fourteen to twenty-one; and adult, for ages twenty-two and up. Male, female, or coed teams compete in groups of four, the traditional number for a *cayuco* team.

Other popular sports in Panama include horse racing, soccer, dog racing, boxing, and cockfighting (in which roosters trained to fight). There is also an abundance of other leisure sports, which take advantage of the country's natural climes and surroundings while catering to the tourist sector. Sports such as surfing, scuba diving, yachting, tennis, golf, and even white-water rafting all draw in Panamanians and tourists alike to partake in Panama's beautiful scenery while doing something exciting and fun.

FOOD IN PANAMA

Just as memorable for visitors to Panama is the country's food. Though Panama is a crossroads of the world, which makes it home to foods from around the globe, there are still types of cuisine that are distinctly Panamanian. Traditional Panamanian cooking is called *comida typica* and usually centers around rice, beans, or lentils served with chicken or fish. In fact, Panama's national dish is *arroz con pollo*, or rice with chicken. *Arroz con pollo* is usually served with any number of added spices, vegetables, or other foods depending on where it is eaten. Other dishes, called *fritura,* are a combination of fried foods. A good example is the Panama-style tortilla, which is a half-inch thick and is made of deep-fried corn dough. They are usually served with melted cheese and eggs and are eaten for breakfast. Also for breakfast are *hojaldras,* flat donuts sprinkled with sugar.

For lunch or dinner, there is *sancocho*, a chicken soup made with the *namé* root. In 2003 Panama City celebrated its one hundredth anniversary by making the largest bowl of *sancocho* ever—2,003 gallons, which went into the *Guinness Book of World Records.* There is also corvina, which is a type of sea bass served in many Panamanian restaurants with shrimp and lobster. Red snapper is also a popular fish to eat. Panama's restaurants also usually serve prawns, similar to shrimp, which is also one of Panama's biggest exports. There are also Panamanian tamales, which look like a square burrito and are filled with chicken or pork. Panamanian tamales differ from most other tamales because they are rolled in a banana leaf rather than a corn husk.

Panama's desserts are just as varied and even more delicious. Flan, which is custard baked in a dish until its sauce caramelizes (sugar hardens on the top), is very popular.

Three-milk cakes are just as sweet and, as the name suggests, are made from three types of milk: evaporated, condensed, and regular. Another dessert is the *batido*, a milk shake made with fresh tropical fruits, milk, and sugar instead of ice cream. And because of its hot climate, Panama is also home to several street vendors selling the one refreshing dessert most often associated with long, hot, humid days—snow cones. In Panama, they are called *raspados*. The word *raspado* literally means "scraped," referring to the method of shaving ice to create light snow-cone flakes.

Drinks are also an important part of Panamanian cuisine. One universal drink that Panama shares with the rest of the

A street vendor prepares a raspado, *a snow cone made of shaved ice.*

world is coffee. Panamanians usually drink coffee espresso-style (very strong and black). The weaker kind of coffee that Americans usually drink is also served but is called *café americano*. Most drinks in Panama, however, are served cold due to the hot climate. The most popular cold drink is beer. Several breweries operate in Panama, producing a variety of beers that many Panamanians drink regularly for refreshment and with meals. One drink that is not as universal as coffee and beer is the *chicha*. *Chichas* are made from fresh tropical fruits blended with ice and water and served in a paper cone similar to a *raspado*. In the Comarca de San Blas, *chichas* are made as alcoholic ceremonial drinks—made from fermented sugarcane juice and flavored with coffee. The *pipa* is another popular drink in Panama. It is a green coconut filled with ice-cold coconut milk and is usually served with a straw.

THE FOODS OF INDIGENOUS TRIBES

The Panamanian Indians have their own cuisine. The food of indigenous tribes such as the Embera and the Wounaan is often simple but quite various. Most tribes use fish from coastal waters or rivers as a main source of protein but supplement this with other meats by hunting iguanas, monkeys, and deer. These people also hunt many of the large rodents that roam the jungles of Panama, such as the *conejo pintado*, whose name means "painted rabbit." This rodent is about the size of a small dog, has brown fur with white spots on its back, and is similar in shape to a rabbit. Meat such as this is hard to find in many areas, however, and so in many poor villages it is only used for special occasions.

Corn, rice, and beans are the staples of many indigenous tribes' diets. They supplement these with limes, oranges, mangos, and other fruits. One of the most important fruits for many Panamanian tribes is the *pixbae*. The *pixbae*, sometimes called a *pifa*, is a fruit about the size of a peach that tastes similar to a chestnut. It grows in the tops of huge palm trees. These giant palms reach heights of up to about one hundred feet, about the same height as a ten story building. Many indigenous tribes have learned to skillfully climb to the tops of these trees in order to harvest the *pixbaes*. When Europeans first reached Panama, Spanish soldiers tried to wipe out the Indians by cutting down the giant palms. The *pixbae* has made a comeback, but it is still a relatively unknown food in much of the world outside the tropics.

From the darkest jungles of Darién to Panama City restaurants, Panamanians enjoy an array of unique cuisines and drinks. Panamanians in small towns without restaurants will often fix visitors meals in their homes for a small price, giving them a chance to show off their variety and skill. Whatever the name or method, food in Panama continues to be a source of pride for its inhabitants and a delight for visitors who come to experience what Panamanian cuisine has to offer.

COMMERCE

Panama also participates in numerous aspects of trade. At all levels, from village bartering to international trade between continents, Panama is witness to a lively and dizzying array of commerce.

The labor force in Panama numbers 1.1 million people. The largest portion of this force is employed in the service sector, which relies heavily on the Panama Canal and its port cities, Panama City and Colón. Some of the major service areas include the actual operation of the canal, banking, insurance, flagship registry, and tourism. Seventy-six percent of the workforce makes up the service sector, while industry accounts for 17 percent. Industries in Panama include construction, petroleum refining, construction-material manufacturing, and sugar milling.

Agriculture is also a large industry in Panama. Some of the most popular crops are bananas, shrimp, and coffee. Other areas of agriculture include rice, corn, sugarcane, vegetables, and livestock. Bananas, shrimp, and coffee, along with sugar, also account for the greatest portion of Panamanian exports. These exports are shipped mainly to the United States. Some 45.9 percent of all Panamanian exports are shipped to the United States, while Costa Rica (5.1 percent); Benelux, the economic union consisting of Belgium, Luxembourg, and the Netherlands (5.3 percent); and Sweden (8.1 percent) are the next-largest importers of Panamanian goods.

Panama also imports a lot of supplies from the United States. Thirty-three percent of imports come from the United States, and roughly another 20 percent come from Ecuador, Venezuela, and Japan. Capital goods (raw materials imported for making other goods), foodstuffs, consumer goods, crude oil, and chemicals are among the largest commodities imported by Panama.

Due to this trade, transportation on the isthmus is abundant, taking many forms. Over two hundred miles of railway crisscross the country. And although the Panama Railroad fell out of use, the newly formed Panama Canal Railway Company has given it new life. In addition, though the majority of Panama's roads are unpaved, it does boast an impressive 7,200 miles of highway. There are also one hundred and three airports, though the majority of those—sixty-two—are also unpaved. Panama also has about five hundred rivers and 1,550 miles of coastline, which means that goods such as crops, textiles, and medicines are also transported by boats to many of the villages and cities throughout the isthmus.

Although the acquisition of the Panama Canal at the end of 1999 resulted in even more positions in the service sector for Panamanian citizens, particularly governmental positions, the unemployment rate continues to be a major source of woe for the country. As of 2002 the unemployment rate was estimated to be at 14 percent. Part of this high unemployment is due to an overly large unskilled workforce, and there remains a shortage of skilled workers to fill positions in all divisions of labor. This predicament also contributes to the large amount of the population below the poverty line—some 37 percent.

Panama, however, continues to adapt and grow. Economic growth was slowed somewhat by international uncertainty during the transition of the operation of the canal from the United States to the Panamanian government. But the government has implemented tax reforms and public work programs and has developed its tourist trade in order to combat the lull and promote growth.

INTERNATIONAL TRADE

One way Panama hopes to grow as a country is through international trade. The United States is Panama's biggest investment and trading partner. Many observers believe that Panama's financial problems may be solved by signing a free-trade agreement with the United States. This would open Panama to new trade opportunities and incoming businesses, creating new jobs for Panamanians and creating an inflow of capital into the country. Although talks have begun to this end, no official word has been given. But Panama is not deterred. The Panamanian government has also begun discussing free-trade agreements with Mexico and the rest of Central America.

As the year 2005 approaches, talk of a free-trade agreement becomes even more important to the United States and Panama. The Free Trade Area of the Americas (FTAA) is scheduled to find a permanent home in Panama in 2005. The FTAA will include thirty-four countries (all the countries of North, South, and Central America, minus Cuba), will cater to a market of possibly 800 million consumers, and will amass revenues of $14 trillion. Panama has been the temporary home of the FTAA since 2000, but a permanent home on the isthmus would almost certainly mean an influx of wealth for the tiny country.

A massive container ship makes its way through the Panama Canal. More than fourteen thousand vessels cross the canal each year.

Panama believes itself to be the proper permanent home for such a huge investment as the FTAA. For the Panamanian government, the Colón free-trade zone and canal are examples of similar earlier success. The canal serves over fourteen thousand vessels a year sailing on over 160 different routes. The Colón free-trade zone does more than $9.5 billion in business per year and contains five private ports and its own airport hub serving nineteen countries. A report by InternationalReports.net, a subsidiary of the *Washington Times*, endorses Panama's bid to host the FTAA, stating, "Perhaps the most commonly named reason for making Panama the permanent FTAA venue is that it is a neutral country with excellent relations in the hemisphere, and therefore a natural candidate to host the hemispheric integration process."[13]

Not all voices are so reassuring, however. Some critics worry that Panama will become nothing but a place for foreign businesses to set up systems of trade. They fear this will further exploit the Panamanian people by replacing their businesses with foreign ones. Whatever the outcome, whether for better or worse, present-day Panama is almost certainly about to change.

The People
of Panama

5

The people of Panama are a diverse mix of nationalities, cultural practices, languages, and customs. Panama's diversity of people is due in large part to its role as a crossroads between the Americas and between the Pacific and Atlantic oceans. International trading in Panama's ports brought in by the Panama Canal has drawn in a wide range of people who now call Panama their home.

Ethnic Groups

Because of the isthmus's role as a passageway for the world, Panama is as ethnically diverse as many other larger countries. The most accurate and recent tally divides the country into four major ethnic groups. The largest group, the mestizos (people of mixed American Indian and European ancestry), make up 70 percent of the population. Another group, blacks with mixed West Indian and American Indian ancestry, make up 14 percent. Most of these West Indian blacks are called Antilleans because the West Indies are also called the Antilles. Whites of predominantly European descent make up 10 percent of the population. Full-blooded American Indians make up about 6 percent. Also accounting for a very small percentage of the population are foreigners from all over the world: Chinese, Jews, Arabs, Greeks, South Asians, Lebanese, western Europeans, and North Americans.

Though Panamanians can be divided by different nationalities, they are divided more noticeably by other traits. These divisions run deeper than just ancestry and include such traits as skin color, living practices, and language.

Whites and culturally integrated Indians are grouped into the mestizo population. The word "mestizo" simply means a person of mixed racial ancestry, but the mestizo population of Panama is largely made up of people of mixed European,

A group of indigenous women from the Kuna Yala tribe pose in vibrantly colored traditional dress.

mainly Spanish, and American Indian blood. Most mestizos are also characterized by the fact that they speak Spanish, which is the official language of Panama. American Indians, descendants of those Indians who inhabited Panama before the European settlers, are separated from the mestizo population because many of them still live in tribal communities and wear tribal dress. An even bigger factor in their separation from mainstream Panama is the language barrier. Every Indian tribe has its own language, and many of the people belonging to these tribes often only speak their tribal tongue.

RELIGION

Panama's religions are as diverse as the people who practice them. The national constitution provides for religious freedom, and thus, most Panamanian citizens worship freely in the religion of their choice. For this reason, Panama continues to grow as a religiously diverse culture.

Roman Catholicism is the largest religion in Panama. A study conducted in 1998 found that 82 percent of Panamanians identify themselves as Roman Catholic. Roman Catholicism was the official religion of Spain when Spanish settlers populated Panama in the 1500s, and Catholicism has remained the predominant religion ever since. Mestizos make up almost all of the Catholic population. Panama's constitution recognizes Catholicism as the predominant faith but stops short of declaring it the state religion, though it does declare that Catholicism be taught in public schools. And while most public schools do teach Catholicism as part of their curriculum, parents are allowed to exempt their children from this part of the instruction. In the mid-1980s Catholics made up almost 90 percent of the population. Their decline over the years has been due in large part to Catholics who have converted to various denominations of Protestantism. Members of the Catholic Church range throughout all levels of the social and economic spectrum, from the wealthy and powerful to the poor.

The next-largest religious group in Panama, Protestants, makes up about 10 percent of the population. Because Protestants, also known as evangelicals, are Christian, they have been allowed to grow without much animosity from the Catholic Church. Protestantism, like Catholicism, has spread throughout Panama, though its members tend to be from the lower economic classes. The bulk of Protestant membership is made up of the Antillean black community, and has its largest followings throughout the provinces of Panama and Colón.

Many other religions are practiced throughout Panama as well. Mormons—members of the Church of Jesus Christ of Latter-day Saints—number about thirty-four thousand people. There are also Seventh-Day Adventists and Episcopalians. Jehovah's Witnesses have around ten thousand members. The Jewish community, concentrated largely in Panama City, is made up of a generally wealthier economic section of the population and accounts for more than seven thousand people. Muslims living in Panama number around five thousand and live mostly in Colón, with some pockets of concentration in David and other cities.

ANTILLEAN BLACKS

Antillean blacks, or West Indian blacks, are separated by more than just skin color from mestizos in Panama, and their history is wrought with the effects of this division. This group originates from the West Indies, which is an archipelago, or group of islands, that stretches about twenty-five hundred miles from Florida to Venezuela. These islands are also called the Antilles. Most of the blacks in Panama have origins in what are known as the Greater Antilles, which include Jamaica, Haiti, and Puerto Rico. Author Richard F. Nyrop explains the origins of Antillean blacks in Panama:

> Black laborers from the British West Indies came to Panama by the tens of thousands in the first half of the twentieth century. Most were involved in the effort to improve the isthmus transportation system, but many came to work on the country's banana plantations as well. By 1910, the Panama Canal Company had employed more than 50,000 workers, three-quarters of whom were Antillean blacks. They formed the nucleus of a community separated from the larger society by race, language, religion, and culture.[14]

Many Antillean blacks in Panama, like these children, lack opportunity, and the Afro-Antillean community continues to struggle for social equality.

Because of their status as an immigrant population, West Indians were and still are somewhat looked down upon by a large portion of the Panamanian mestizo population. The men and women sometimes known as Afro-Antilleans were exploited as cheap labor on the railroads and canal. Afro-Antilleans spoke mainly English. This was because they were from islands that were colonized by England or because they had received educations from American schools in the Canal Zone. For these same reasons, a large part of them also became Protestants, the dominant religion in both the United States and Britain. This became another reason they have been looked down upon. All of these factors continue to be impediments in the Antillean blacks' struggle for social equality in Panama, and racism against the Afro-Antillean community remains a problem in Panama today.

THE INDIGENOUS PEOPLES OF PANAMA

The indigenous peoples of Panama make up approximately 6 percent of the population. In all, they can be divided into six major tribes, though because of similarities in a few, they are just as often grouped into four. The indigenous tribes of Panama are the Kuna, the Guaymi, the Embera, the Wounaan, the Teribe, and the Bokota. Because of their cultural similarities and the fact that they live close to each other, the Embera and the Wounaan are usually grouped together, as are the Teribe and the Bokota.

The indigenous cultures of Panama have been struggling for nearly five hundred years, ever since the first Spanish explorers arrived. Several cultures were lost to genocidal practices and to Spanish integration. Over the centuries, indigenous tribes have gone from fighting for their survival to fighting for their land and culture. But their progress has been slow. Only recently, in the year 2000, did the Legislative Assembly pass Act No. 20, which stated that the way of life for indigenous tribes was protected by law. Under this new law, the "customs, traditions, beliefs, spirituality, religion, cosmic view, folkloric expressions, artistic manifestations, traditional knowledge and all other traditional forms of expression of indigenous peoples are protected."[15] The act was an attempt by the Panamanian government to acknowledge the rich indigenous heritage that is still prevalent in the mixture of today's Panamanian culture.

BODY ART, ANCIENT AND CONTEMPORARY

Art in indigenous Panamanian culture dates back to well before Spanish explorers and settlers landed on the Atlantic coast. The type of work for which ancient tribes were most famous was their goldwork. Tribal craftsmen would beat the soft metal into thin pliable sheets to be worked into bracelets, earrings, and chest plates. Nobility would often possess such accoutrements as gold headbands and necklaces. There is evidence that many tribes even learned how to melt and mold gold into small objects and figures.

The same kind of metalwork and craftsmanship still exists today in the art of the Embera and the Wounaan. Women and men often wear long gold or silver bracelets and arm and ankle bands. Necklaces made out of coins are sometimes worn for special ceremonies and celebrations.

Men and women also adorn themselves in *jagua* body paint. The *jagua* is a fruit that has long been used by both the Wounaan and the Embera. According to age and gender, black *jagua* dye is applied to the skin in certain patterns. Sometimes this is done in solid blocks and at other times in patterns painted on with a thin tip of bamboo. Native Planet, a Web site about indigenous peoples, describes the process:

> [First the *jagua* fruit] needs to be grated. The pulp is then mixed with a very small amount of water and squeezed by hand or inside a piece of fabric to extract a liquid that darkens as it oxidizes. To make it stronger, the liquid is often heated in a pan over a fire. . . . Then the jagua juice is ready to be applied directly on dry skin. It dries in minutes and the indelible markings cannot be removed with any type of soap, detergent or chemicals. It remains in the skin until the upper layer of skin is naturally exfoliated [flaked off] by the body.

THE KUNA

A rich example of indigenous culture in Panama is the Kuna tribe. The Kuna (also Cuna), sometimes known as the Dule or Tule tribe, is the second-largest tribe in Panama with a little under fifty thousand members. They are the most powerful tribe and the only tribe to control a completely autonomous region. This was the first such region created completely for an indigenous people and was acknowledged by the Panamanian government in 1938. The region where they live is known as the Comarca de San Blas. It is also called simply Kuna Yala or Dulenega by the Kuna. Now, the region operates like its own province, almost completely separate from the Panamanian government. Twice a year, three

A young Kuna girl poses with her parrot. The Kuna tribe lives in the dense tropical rain forest, and their isolation has helped preserve their traditional culture.

elected caciques, or *sahila* (chiefs), lead a general congress in which community matters are discussed.

The Kuna are the oldest present-day inhabitants of the isthmus. They are believed by anthropologists to have inhabited parts of the San Blas archipelago and Darién Province as early as ten thousand years ago. Their culture has been largely protected from outside influence by surrounding swamps, dense tropical rain forest, and the San Blas Range to the south. As a result, their language, customs, and genetics remain the purest examples of an indigenous population in Panama.

The society of the Kuna is matriarchal, which means that inheritances pass through the women instead of the men. Upon marrying, young men must move into the house of their mother-in-law and apprentice with their father-in-law. Daughters are prized over sons because of their ability to produce children. Traditionally, labor is divided by gender. A husband gathers coconuts, performs repairs on the house, collects firewood, and makes clothes for his sons. Wives pre-

THE STORY OF THE *MOLA*

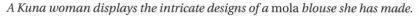

In Kuna villages, a town crier shouts out, "*Mormaknamaloe.*" It means, "Go sew *molas.*" Upon hearing this call, women of the village go to a meeting place and wait for the village chief to chant the story of the *mola* and the two most important women in Kuna history, Kikkatiriyai and Nagagiriyai.

Kikkatiriyai was a Kuna woman who lived during the first century A.D. She organized a school in which she taught other women of her village how to make cloth out of tree bark and other plants by soaking them in water and softening them. As the story goes, much later Nagagiriyai, a female seer (woman who could foresee future events), known as a *nele*, discovered the *mola* in a dream and was transported to a mythical place that only women were able to enter. Inside, she saw on the white rock walls all the geometric and colorful designs that were to be made by the Kuna women and memorized them. She taught the Kuna women these designs upon her return, which were then put onto all kinds of items of clothing, but most of all the *molas.*

A Kuna woman displays the intricate designs of a mola *blouse she has made.*

pare food, clean the house, gather fresh water, unload boats, and make clothes for the women of the family.

Kuna women have retained their traditional dress much more than the men have, and their clothing is often a spectacular array of vibrant colors. Among their dress is the traditional *mola* blouse, which is adorned with two brilliantly patterned *molas* (panels of layered cloth woven together to form pictures and geometric patterns). The women believe that *molas* embody the spirit of their designs, which range from gods and animals to simple nature patterns. The two *molas* on a blouse, though different, are usually united by the same theme. The *mola* became a commercial item when tourists began buying used *molas* from Kuna women— whenever a Kuna woman grows tired of her design, she removes the *molas* from her blouse and sews on another pair with a different theme. This has led to the making of *molas* specifically for sale to tourists. These tourist *molas* have none of the history, artisanship, or personal quality that makes the bright authentic *molas* of the Kuna women so special and distinct.

This increasing tourism has had its influence on other aspects of Kuna culture as well. Tourists have brought with them an influx of Western-style goods, particularly clothing such as baseball caps and jerseys displaying the names of sports teams, which many Kuna males now wear. Also, U.S. dollar bills are often accepted to buy fish and other goods. This is very different from the Kuna's other form of currency, the coconut. The coconut is one of the main commodities in the Comarca de San Blas and accounts for a large portion of income to the Kuna tribe. Because of their system of bartering and the abundance of coconuts, the coconut became a common form of payment among the Kuna people. The Kuna still sell or barter around 30 million coconuts a year, mostly to Colombians.

Although they have been exposed to other cultures, the Kuna have remained distinct. Despite missionary efforts to Christianize them, the predominant Kuna religion is still animism, which means they believe that all natural objects are inhabited by some kind of spirit. The Kuna have also barred outsiders from being integrated into their culture by marrying only within the tribe. The penalty for marrying outside of the tribe is exile. By keeping foreigners out of their affairs and families, the Kuna ensure that the profits from businesses like hotels and souvenir sales stay within the tribe. Their fishing practices and coconut harvesting do not disturb the environment, and ancient cultural rites and beliefs are retained. To this day, the Kuna remain the strongest indigenous tribe in resisting assimilation into Spanish-influenced Panamanian culture. In fact, the Kuna have inspired greater political influence and more acknowledged rights for other indigenous cultures in Panama.

THE GUAYMI

The Guaymi inhabit the semiautonomous region known as the Ngobe-Buglé Comarca (other names for the Guaymi tribe are the Ngobe and the Ngwobe), an indigenous region spanning parts of the provinces of Veraguas, Bocas del Toro, and Chiriquí, a considerably large portion of land that makes up about 9 percent of Panama. The Guaymi tribe is by far the largest in Panama with a population of around 125,000. Unlike the Kuna, the Guaymi live under Panamanian law, and most Guaymi children attend Panamanian public schools.

A Guaymi family walks through their village. The Guaymi tribe is the largest in Panama, with a population of nearly 125,000.

GUAYMI FESTIVALS

The Guaymi Indians of Panama regularly celebrate many of their traditions. Every year, between October and February, many members of the Guaymi tribe come to the coffee-growing region of Boquete to help harvest its world-famous coffee crop. During this time the Guaymi celebrate the coming together of their various members with a series of festivals.

A large part of these festivals is the Guaymi music. Members of the Guaymi tribe are very musical and play a variety of instruments, such as the conch shell, called a *drù*; and a mouth harp known as a *truma*, which is used to start communal gatherings and to welcome friends. The *tolero*, a small flutelike instrument, can also be used for calling such gatherings and other events, including the *krün* (also known as the *balseria*) and the *chichería*. Javier Montezuma, a writer for the Amazon Conservation Team, explains the *chichería* and the *jegui* of the Guaymi people: "The Jegui, that takes place during a party known as chichería, is the traditional dance of the [Guaymi] people. All take part, men, women, youth and even children. The singers start with four youths and slowly more dancers join in until a great circle is formed moving in zigzags, like the manta ray, the sacred fish of the Ngäbe people. The elders dedicate a song known as Guara to this fish."

At these festivities, a number of traditional games are also played. The *krün* is a game played by Guaymi men that consists of men attempting to hit each other in the calf with balsa wood poles, or *balsos*, from a distance of about ten feet. The game has ancient origins and coincided with the harvest of maize and peach palm each year, much the same way it does today with the coffee harvest. Originally, the *krün* was part of a large drunken festivity between two tribes in which the two chiefs would play the opponents. Due to the game's sometimes violent nature (the game takes place all day, and a victory is accomplished when the loser falls down from pain—in a few instances the loser has even died), Panama's government declared the event illegal. And even though some Guaymi tribes have since quit the practice, it still exists among others.

Guaymi Indians like these men play traditional games and a variety of musical instruments during their festivals.

The Guaymi tribe was once a warrior culture, but the
Guaymi were forced to seek refuge in isolated pockets of
western Panama in order to escape Spanish soldiers during
Spain's occupation of the isthmus. For this reason, the
Guaymi were and still are divided into two distinct groups.
One group took refuge in the highland rain forest of the
Cordillera Central. The other group settled in the lowlands
along the Atlantic coast. Even when Panama became part of
Colombia during the nineteenth century, the Guaymi had
isolated themselves in the mountains to such a point that
they remained unaware of the transfer of government. Being
isolated and spread out also caused a separation between
several Guaymi communities. As a result, at least five different Guaymi languages are spoken among the tribes.

The Ngobe-Buglé Comarca consists of around twenty-five
hundred square miles of land; about half of it is farmable.
Using the land has been an important part of the Guaymi
culture and history. Centuries ago, the Guaymi often settled
on hilltops as a way to watch for attacking Spanish troops.
There was little chance for hunting or gathering in these areas, and thus the Guaymi became capable farmers. This heritage has been passed down through the centuries and still
remains an important part of the culture. To this day, the
Guaymi practice eco-friendly, long-term, sustainable farming techniques.

THE EMBERA AND THE WOUNAAN

The Embera tribe has an estimated population of around fifteen thousand and inhabits portions of Darién Province.
They are often grouped with the Wounaan tribe (estimated
population around two thousand) because both groups are
believed to have migrated northwest sometime between the
1600s and the 1700s from the Choco region of Colombia; because of this, they are also commonly called Choco Indians.
Some experts suggest, however, that both tribes were in
Panama even before the Spanish conquistadors. They theo-
rize that Europeans had simply not noticed them until the
seventeenth century, which is when the first serious foreign
explorations of Darién took place.

Not much is known about the origins of either tribe because they have no early written history. All histories were
oral in both tribes until relatively recently. In addition, both

tribes relied on hunting and fishing for good portions of their food sources, which caused them to be semi-nomadic, often living in small groups of only a few families and moving with their food sources to where game was abundant. Such a culture has left very little evidence behind for anthropologists interested in tracing Embera and Wounaan origins.

In 1983 the government of Panama recognized both tribes' rights to what is now called the Comarca Embera-Drua, a semiautonomous region lying within two protected areas, Darién National Park and the 1.5-million-acre Darién Biosphere Reserve, which is the largest protected area in Panama and one of the largest in Central America. The recognition was due to an organizational alliance of the Embera and the Wounaan in an attempt to protect their homelands and rights as indigenous cultures.

Children of the Embera tribe wear bright beads and body paint. The Embera have worked with the Panamanian government to help protect their homeland.

The Embera and the Wounaan have become two of the strongest opponents of finishing the Pan-American Highway. Both tribes have always led a hunter-gatherer way of life,

which means that instead of farming, they hunt wild game and gather wild plants and fruits in order to sustain themselves. In 1979, however, the Pan-American Highway made Darién accessible to slash-and-burn farmers. These farmers cut down and burned trees in order to plant crops and raise cattle, decimating huge swaths of rain forest. The rain forests decreased in size, and thus the Embera and the Wounaan could no longer live on the amount of wild game or plants they found. As a result, the Embera and the Wounaan were forced to resort to slash-and-burn farming as well because this was the only kind of agriculture they knew. Realizing that this could not continue, the tribes fought back. In a show of solidarity, the Embera and Wounaan tribes, along with the Guaymi and the Kuna, announced in 1995 official opposition to plans for finishing the Pan-American Highway. The road remains unfinished. Despite the victory, however, the small Wounaan tribe separated once again from the Embera in 1998, feeling it was not being fairly represented by the interests of the majority.

THE TERIBE AND THE BRIBRI

To the west, along the Costa Rican border, lives the Teribe tribe, which has a small population of around two thousand. This tribe is also called the Naso, which is how they refer to themselves. They live among the forests along the Teribe River, which continues to be an isolated area.

The Teribe live in twenty-seven communities in Bocas del Toro Province. Their government is led by a *pru*, or king, and is governed by a council of thirty members. The Teribe tribe subsists mainly through its agriculture, growing platano, corn, cocoa, coffee, jobo, guanabana, pineapple guayaba, oranges, and lemons. They also raise chickens and turkeys. Hunting is done with bows and arrows and sometimes rifles to kill mainly rabbits. The Teribe add to their income by making hammocks and baskets to sell.

One additional group of indigenous people in Panama is the Bribri tribe. The Bribri, part of the Costa Rican Talamanca tribe, crossed the Costa Rican border sometime during the twentieth century to find work on Panamanian banana plantations. Only about five hundred Bribri live in Panama today.

THE FUTURE: PROBLEMS FACING PANAMA

During the twentieth century Panama emerged as a country complete with all the international problems, fiscal responsibilities, economic worries, and ecological concerns of much older nations. Though Panama seems to be gaining ground as a stable nation, it may be difficult to free itself from many of its problems. Panama still struggles to overcome its long, turbulent history of military and political corruption. And these problems may only hinder its ability to respond to a constant drug-trafficking problem coming from its border with Colombia.

As with many countries, however, Panama's economic problems are its most formidable obstacles. It is true that Panama continues to expand its role as an international crossroads and area of trade. But if money does not find its way into the domestic economy, the already large poor population will grow. Indeed, Panama's future will depend on how it deals with the problems of today so they do not become insurmountable in the future.

POLITICAL CORRUPTION

Despite the fact that democracy has gained strength and stability in Panama, much of the government continues to operate corruptly. Practices of the old oligarchy, such as nepotism (favoritism to relatives) are still common. Many of the people from wealthy and powerful families still hire one another in order to retain control over the government while using their influence to keep their political enemies out of power. This corruption in the government extends into all sectors. In 2003 seven members of the state-owned National Hypothecating Bank were fired for erasing the debts of their

Protesters demonstrate against the termination of Panama's National Security Fund director in 2003.

relatives. That same year, well-connected elites were discovered to have used three hundred thousand gallons of plane fuel belonging to the National Air Service tanks, which service the air force division of the National Police as well as presidential aircraft, to fuel their private helicopters and planes free of charge.

However, corrupt Panamanian politics are now protested regularly by the people. The working classes no longer live under a military dictatorship and thus have more freedom to express themselves. In September 2003 the nation's teachers and several Social Security employees went on strike. Then, among a group of one hundred thousand protesters, marched to a main square in Panama City to refute what they thought to be the unjust dismissal of the country's National Security Fund director for his stance against some of the president's policies.

Corruption is not only confined to Panama's political elite. There is evidence that corrupt practices have trickled down into all aspects of Panamanian life. Journalist Michelle Lescure states how universal corruption has become:

> For centuries, corruption has been viewed in Latin America as a way of getting things done. Almost all Latin

WIDENING THE CANAL

The Panama Canal is once again a source of major debate in Panama. The Panamanian government has begun to consider a project to add a third, wider set of locks to the canal in order to accommodate the growing number of seafaring freighters, called "post-Panamax vessels," that are too large to pass through the Panama Canal.

The old locks are made to accommodate ships carrying up to sixty-five thousand tons of cargo, but today some cargo ships are capable of carrying three hundred thousand tons. Even some cruise ships are now becoming too big for the locks. According to the Panamanian government, the lock project is estimated to cost $200 million.

The talks concerning the locks are part of what is estimated to become a $1-billion expansion project for the canal. The Panamanian government hopes the spending will be justified. Government officials estimate that an expansion to accommodate the majority of freight vessels in the world would increase the number of boats passing through the Panama Canal from fourteen thousand to sixteen thousand ships a year, bringing in almost 20 percent more revenue.

But beyond the question of money are the technical, public, and ecological concerns regarding a new set of locks. The locks would almost assuredly mean that whole groups of people would be displaced by the man-made lake that would be required to provide water for the locks. In addition, the effects of such a large project on the ecology of surrounding rain forest could be ecologically devastating. Therefore, the canal's expansion remains a topic of debate for Panamanians.

American citizens have become accomplices in one way or another—in order to obtain a driver's license or a telephone line, to expedite the retrieval of a package at the post office or customs, or to supplement an insufficient income. Others have obtained university degrees, enriched their personal fortunes, avoided prosecution or imprisonment, used government resources to win elections, laundered illegal funds, managed lucrative illegal drug or arms trafficking operations, or have benefited in some other way from corruption.[16]

No area of Panamanian life, political or personal, large-scale or small, it would seem, is free from corruption. Carlos Quintanilla Schmidt, the vice president of El Salvador, summed up the epidemic of corruption in Panama and all of Latin America when he said, "Corruption has become an anti-value and the corrupt, because of their astuteness and 'success,' are admired and emulated by both the rich and poor."[17]

CRIME

Panama faces problems with crime at every level, corruption being only one problem. International travelers visiting Panama are warned about the eastern side of Darién along the Colombian border because of dangerous criminal activity there. An information sheet published by the U.S. Department of State warns, "While no incidents have occurred at [private resorts], U.S. citizens, other foreign nationals and Panamanian citizens have been the victims of violent crime, kidnapping and murder in this area."[18]

Violent crimes such as these are due largely to drug traffickers, common thieves, and Colombian terrorist groups roaming the Darién jungles. The Revolutionary Armed Forces of Colombia, National Liberation Army, and United Self-Defense Forces of Colombia have all been deemed foreign terrorist organizations by the United States. These groups operate within Darién along a large area of land that stretches along the Colombian border. It is difficult to fight crime in this region, however, because it is so remote. In 2003 Panama received $4 million in aid from the United States to help deal with this problem. This money will help build roads, buildings, and otherwise modernize areas in Darién to more effectively police Colombian drug activity and violence.

Though not as dangerous as the Colombian border, Panama City is also an area where crime is growing. Crime is even higher in the city of Colón outside of the free-trade zone. Most of the crime in these cities is caused by a growing number of youth gangs, which have begun using an increased number of illegal weapons. Armed violence has risen in almost all metropolitan areas.

Panamanian police officers inspect confiscated weapons. Armed violence, predominately by gangs, has been increasing throughout the cities of Panama.

A Panamanian teenager rides his bicycle through a slum of Colón. Poverty is a huge problem for many areas of Panama.

Crimes committed in these areas include rapes, muggings, and purse snatchings. Another now-common form of crime has become known as "express kidnapping," in which thieves wait near ATMs for tourists and citizens to make withdrawals, then kidnap them for a brief time while they rob them of their money. In an attempt to curb the activity of these youth gangs, in 1996 Panama City implemented a curfew for people under the age of eighteen. Children caught roaming the streets after curfew are taken into police custody; their parents are then subject to fines of up to fifty dollars. While this has deterred some youth gangs, the real problem in crime-ridden urban areas such as Colón and parts of Panama City remains the poverty levels among the low economic classes.

POVERTY

Poverty continues to be a problem in several areas of Panama. A study by the World Bank in 1999 showed that more than 1 million people, about 37 percent of Panama's population, were living below the poverty line. The poverty line is defined as a level of income below which a person no longer has adequate means to sustain himself or herself in acceptable living conditions. Among these poor, about half a million, or almost 19 percent of the population, were found to be living in extreme poverty. Poverty accounts for almost all cases of malnutrition in Panama. Sixteen percent of all Panamanian children under the age of five suffer from some form of malnutrition.

There are a number of different reasons why poverty persists. Job options for the poor, especially in urban areas, are limited due to a lack of education. Also, nearly three-fourths of the poor in Panama work at informal jobs—these are jobs that take place outside the normal rules of business set up by the government. Informal jobs, then, are not protected by laws regulating minimum wage or work hours. Thus, the poor working in informal jobs on average earn about half what those in the public and private sector make. Another element that adds to the problem is discrimination. Studies show that indigenous groups, women, and youths in poor communities all have considerably fewer employment opportunities.

Rural areas account for the majority—nearly three-fourths —of Panama's poor population. Nearly eight hundred thousand people live in poverty in rural communities. The largest portion of the rural poor is made up of the indigenous tribes of Panama. The Guaymi, the Embera, and the Wounaan make up the biggest section of indigenous poor. This problem is only made worse by the fact that indigenous tribes have a high fertility rate, meaning they reproduce more than other ethnic groups in Panama. Part of this is due to the fact that children are an important part of the indigenous culture, helping to replenish the farming workforce and community. However, it also means more and more children are being born into poverty in indigenous tribes.

As a result of such poverty, these areas are plagued by a lack of education, underemployment, and an inability to sustain acceptable levels of food. On August 4, 2003, a state of emergency was declared for the semiautonomous region of the Ngobe-Buglé Comarca (Guaymi) in which nearly 95 percent of children were malnourished. The Panamanian government is still struggling to modernize many areas in which indigenous tribes suffer from such debilitating poverty. It remains to be seen how and if Panama will meet these persistent problems of its population still living below the poverty line.

DANGER IN PANAMA

Ever since U.S. military presence on the isthmus began almost one hundred years ago, the United States has used land in Panama's Canal Zone for army training and military bases of operation. Sometimes this training meant testing weapons. In 1999 the United States ceded to the Panamanian government more than seventy thousand acres of Canal Zone land, over half of which is said to still contain dangerous military weapons, such as unexploded munitions, including land mines, unused artillery, and other explosive devices.

When U.S. troops left army bases in Panama, they had marked nearly eight hundred different areas as unsafe because of the possibility that dangerous weapons were still there in some form or another. Indeed, by March 2000 Panamanians had been reported killed by these weapons, with several others injured. The victims were often farmers attempting to clear land for crops or even poorer Panamanians just looking for metal to recycle.

Because much of the Canal Zone is made up of dense jungle, the U.S. government claimed that cleaning up the weapons was not possible. But many Panamanian government officials believe that the U.S. government is just trying to save the millions of dollars that need to be spent on cleaning up the weapons.

Many Panamanians also believe that there are chemical weapons left behind in Panama. There is, indeed, documented proof that the U.S. government tested chemical weapons in the Canal Zone at different times throughout its stay in Panama. Panamanian officials are thus concerned for the safety of between sixty to one hundred thousand Panamanian citizens who live near the Canal Zone. The question for the Panamanian government is how to go about dealing with the estimated 110,000 pieces of military ordnance left behind before the growing cities surrounding the Canal Zone put more people in harm's way.

U.S. military forces in Panama have existed for nearly one hundred years.

RACISM

Racism, particularly against blacks, is yet another form of discrimination that has added to social and economic disparity in Panama. Racism against blacks has subsided somewhat in the last half-century, yet racist practices remain in all aspects of Panamanian life. In January 1941 racism on the part of Panamanian citizens led by then-president Arnulfo Arias resulted in the ratification of a new constitution that deprived Afro-Antilleans of Panamanian citizenship. And although Arias was ousted from power the same year, the racist law against non-Hispanics, particularly blacks, stood for five years until it was revoked in 1946. The legacy of such racism is clear today. A report on human rights practices from 2001, released by the U.S. Bureau of Democracy, Human Rights, and Labor, states, "Blacks are conspicuously absent from positions of political and economic power. The country's white elite successfully marginalizes citizens with darker skin through preferential hiring practices in the private sector and manipulation of government resources in the public sector."[19] Specifically, Antillean blacks, easily identifiable from their unique dress and their use of English, are often the subject of racial slurs and poor treatment from other Spanish-speaking black and mestizo citizens alike.

Subject to many of the same racist practices are the country's other minorities–Chinese, East Indians, Middle Eastern Arabs and Jews, Greeks, and Hispanic blacks and Indians. Specifically, Chinese immigrants are the targets of a great deal of racial discrimination. A U.S. state report on Panama says that "racial slurs directed at Asians are used openly among the general population."[20] This occurs because of a few different factors. First, Chinese is very different from Spanish, so many Chinese only learn limited Spanish. The Chinese are also a very large group. More than 120,000 ethnic Chinese live in Panama, most within the major cities. Much like Antillean blacks, most Chinese are easily identifiable, which makes them easy targets for racist Panamanians.

The Chinese are an easy target for many financial problems affecting other Panamanian businesses. Along with Middle Eastern and East Indian residents, the Chinese control much of the retail trade within the country. And for a country that relies heavily on its service sectors, namely those sectors that cater to the canal, this control of retail trade makes them targets of jealousy and hatred among the dominant mestizo population. Thus, the Chinese, along with entrepreneurs from India and other discernible ethnic groups, are often the victims of governmental discrimination as well. This usually comes in the form of bureaucratic difficulties. Government offices sometimes make it intentionally difficult for foreigners to get vending licenses: They stall paperwork and require higher fees from foreigners.

This has led a new form of racism to emerge in Panama—racism against members of one's own race. The Chinese community has experienced such a split. Second- and third-generation Chinese who are now Panamanian citizens and speak Spanish have begun distancing themselves from other newly arrived Chinese or even older members of their own families. This trend proves the power of racism, a problem that will likely continue until Panamanians are willing to accept that their country, as a crossroads of the world, is quickly becoming one of the most racially diverse places on earth.

DRUG TRAFFICKING

Panama's role as a center for international activity has also attracted business of another kind—drug trafficking. However,

Police officers stack kilos of seized cocaine. The country's dense jungles and its proximity to Colombia facilitate drug trafficking in Panama.

most of Panama's drug problems do not originate in Panama. As Representative John L. Mica, a congressman from Florida once noted, "There can be no meaningful discussion of the drug situation in Panama without considering the current happenings in Colombia."[21] Because Panama shares a border with Colombia, many of that nation's problems spill into Panama. Panama's police force has been unable to suitably fight the drug trafficking that goes on along the border with Colombia, a cause for concern among many Panamanians.

The Darién Gap of Panama has particularly become a haven for drug traffickers. Its dense jungles provide the perfect cover for drug production and transportation, and drug dealers working in Colombia can easily slip across the border. Drug dealers have also joined forces with various Colombian paramilitary groups that operate throughout the jungle region. Paramilitary groups are often nothing but groups of Colombians who have armed themselves to fight for political causes. Many such groups have made alliances with drug dealers to finance their operations.

These groups are often malicious, burning villages and slaughtering people in gruesome fashion. One group, known as the Autonomous Defense Units of Colombia (AUC), has gained the nickname "the Head Cutters" because of their tactics. Early in 2003 an AUC group of about 150 men attacked two Kuna villages and killed four leaders, mutilating three of their bodies with machetes. Because of these groups' well-funded and brutal tactics, the drug trade has only increased in Darién. There is evidence now that some indigenous tribes living within the region have even been recruited to work on coca farms to aid in cocaine production.

Mourners grieve over the coffin of a murdered Kuna leader in 2003. Four Kuna leaders were brutally murdered when a paramilitary group attacked their village.

In addition to activity in Darién, Panama has become an ideal place for drug smugglers to launch international drug shipments. There are many reasons for this. First, Panama's coastlines are largely unpatrolled. Second, Panama's judicial systems are still somewhat underdeveloped, making it difficult to prosecute drug-related offenses. Corruption in the government has also allowed drug dealers to bribe their way into the legitimate financial system that continues to grow.

Smugglers continue to find ways of smuggling drugs from Colombia through Panama, usually for shipment into the United States and Mexico. Using speedboats that can travel up to sixty miles per hour (faster than most navy boats), smugglers drop shipments on deserted Panamanian beaches or leave them floating off the coast for pick up. These trips usually take only about twenty minutes. Each boat usually carries at least two tons of cocaine and heroin. Colombian police even found a half-completed seventy-five-foot-long submarine that, had it been completed, would have been able to carry a ten-ton drug shipment. Smugglers also use Global Positioning Systems to meet with fishing boats in open water off Panama's coast. Often, these shipments are smuggled onto freighters carrying cargo from Panama to the United States.

Panama's government has taken steps to prevent this kind of drug trafficking through the country. Since 2000 it has adopted major financial and banking reform laws that allow law enforcement officials to track the flow of illegal money. In 2001 Panama signed an agreement that allows the United States to help patrol the coastal waters off Panama's shores. However, while these measures may help to battle the expanding drug trade and other criminal activity, they cannot completely correct the problems of corruption, racism, and poverty.

In 2003 Panama celebrated its one hundredth anniversary as an independent country. They have been years full of strife, triumph, change, and growth. How the next one hundred years proceed will depend on the ability of the Panamanian people to rise to the challenges facing them now and in the future.

FACTS ABOUT PANAMA

GENERAL INFORMATION

Country name: Republic of Panama

Government type: constitutional democracy

Capital: Panama City

Administrative divisions: nine provinces and one territory (*comarca*)

Independence: November 3, 1903 (from Colombia; became independent from Spain in 1821)

Executive branch: president, elected by popular vote to a five-year term; cabinet, appointed by the president

Legislative branch: unicameral (one house) Legislative Assembly (*Asamblea Legislativa*); seventy-one seats with members elected by popular vote to serve five-year terms

Judicial branch: Supreme Court of Justice (*Corte Suprema de Justicia*), with nine judges appointed for ten-year terms; five superior courts; three courts of appeal

PEOPLE

Population (July 2003): 2,960,784

Age structure (2003): 0–14 years, 30.6% (male 461,670; female 443,671); 15–64 years, 63.3% (male 950,089; female 924,038); 65 years and over, 6.1% (male 86,006; female 95,310)

Population growth rate (2003): 1.36%

Birthrate (2003): 20.78 births per 1,000 population

Death rate (2003): 6.25 deaths per 1,000 population

Infant mortality rate: 21.44 deaths per 1,000 live births

Life expectancy at birth (2003): 72.32 years (male, 69.97 years; female, 74.79 years)

Fertility rate (2003): 2.53 children born per woman

Ethnic groups: mestizo (mixed American Indian and white), 70%; American Indian and mixed (West Indian), 14%; white, 10%; American Indian, 6%

Religions: Roman Catholic, 82%; Protestant, 10%

Languages: Spanish (official); English, 14%; note: many Panamanians are bilingual

Literacy (definition: age 15 and over who can read and write) (2003): total population, 92.6%; male, 93.2%; female, 91.9%

GEOGRAPHY

Area: total, 30,193 square miles; land, 29,339 square miles; water, 854 square miles

Bordering countries: Colombia, Costa Rica

Shores: Caribbean Sea, North Pacific Ocean

Climate: tropical maritime; hot, humid, cloudy; prolonged rainy season (May to January); short dry season (January to May)

Terrain: interior mostly steep, rugged mountains and dissected, upland plains; coastal areas largely plains and rolling hills

Elevation extremes: sea level to 11,400 feet (Chiriquí volcano)

Natural resources (1998): copper, mahogany forests, shrimp, hydropower

Land use: arable land, 6.72 %; permanent crops, 2.08%; other, 91.2%

Natural hazards: occasional severe storms and forest fires in the Darién area

Environmental issues: water pollution from agricultural runoff threatens fishery resources; deforestation of tropical rain forest; land degradation and soil erosion threatens siltation of Panama Canal; air pollution in urban areas; mining threatens natural resources

ECONOMY

Gross domestic product (GDP) (2002): $17.3 billion

GDP growth rate (2002): 0.8%

GDP per capita (2002): $6,000

GDP by sector (2001): agriculture, 7%; industry, 17%; service, 76%

Population below poverty line (1999): 37%

Inflation rate (2001): 1.1%

Labor force (2000): 1.1 million; note: a shortage of skilled labor coexists with an oversupply of unskilled labor

Budget: revenues, $1.9 billion; expenditures, $2 billion

Industries: construction, petroleum refining, brewing, cement and other construction materials, sugar milling

Agricultural products: bananas, rice, corn, coffee, sugarcane, vegetables, livestock, shrimp

Exports (2002): $5.8 billion

Imports (2002): $6.7 billion

Currency: balboa (1 balboa is equal to 1 U.S. dollar)

NOTES

CHAPTER 1: A WORLD UNTO ITSELF

1. Quoted in Peter Eltringham et al. *The Rough Guide to Central America*. New York: Penguin Books, 1999, p. 673.

2. Eltringham, *The Rough Guide to Central America*, p. 659.

CHAPTER 2: FROM SPAIN'S DISCOVERY TO AN INTERNATIONAL PASSAGEWAY

3. Quoted in David Howarth, *Panama: Four Hundred Years of Dreams and Cruelty*. New York: McGraw Hill, 1966, p. 13.

4. Christopher Ward, *Imperial Panama: Commerce and Conflict in Isthmian America, 1550–1800*. Albuquerque: University of New Mexico Press, 1993, p. 47.

5. Quoted in Diane de Gaffenreid, ed., *Panama: Sovereignty for a Land Divided*. Washington, DC: EPICA Task Force, 1976, p. 7.

6. Quoted in Ward, *Imperial Panama*, p. 55.

CHAPTER 3: THE AGE OF INDUSTRY, INDEPENDENCE, AND POLITICS

7. David McCullough, *The Path Between the Seas: The Creation of the Panama Canal, 1870–1914*. New York: Simon and Schuster, 1977, p. 142.

8. McCullough, *The Path Between the Seas*, pp. 545, 611.

9. McCullough, *The Path Between the Seas*, p. 591.

10. The Panama Canal, "This Is the Canal." www.pancanal.com.

11. Tom Barry et al., *Inside Panama: The Essential Guide to Its Politics, Economy, Society, and Environment*. Albuquerque: Resource Center, 1995, p. 33.

CHAPTER 4: PRESENT-DAY PANAMA

12. Barry et al, *Inside Panama.*

13. InternationalReports.net, "Free Trade Agreement with U.S. Is Top Priority." www.internationalreports.net.

CHAPTER 5: THE PEOPLE OF PANAMA

14. U.S. Library of Congress, "The Society and Its Environment" in *Panama: A Country Study*, Richard F. Nyrop, ed. http://countrystudies.us/panama.

15. International Centre for Human Rights and Democratic Development, "Republic of Panama—Act No. 20." www.ichrdd.ca.

CHAPTER 6: THE FUTURE: PROBLEMS FACING PANAMA

16. Michelle Lescure, "Speaking Out Against Corruption," *World Press Review*, April 11, 2002. www.worldpress.org.

17. Quoted in Lescure, "Speaking Out Against Corruption."

18. U.S. Department of State, "Consular Information Sheet: Panama." http://travel.state.gov.

19. Panama Women and Children in Need, "U.S. State Report on Panama." www.panamawomenandchildreninneed.com

20. Panama Women and Children in Need, "U.S. State Report on Panama."

21. Quoted in Rob O'Dell, "Drug Trafficking Up in Panama," June 11, 2000, *Cannabis News*. www.cannabisnews.com.

GLOSSARY

archipelago: a large group of islands

cacique: a tribal chief

campesino: a peasant farmer

canal: a man-made waterway used for transportation or shipping

cayuco: a wooden canoe made from a single tree; usually carved by Choco Indians

cimarrones: fugitive slaves who survived to be part of a community of other escaped slaves in the jungles of Panama

comarca: a region or territory

cordillera: mountain range

ecoregion: a large unit of land or water containing a specific and classifiable habitat, specific wildlife, and having a specific climate

ecotourism: tourism that concerns itself with preserving the place of interest and its wildlife

forty-niners: people who took part in the rush to California in search of gold in 1849

fritura: panamanian fried foods

hojaldra: a kind of flat donut usually sprinkled with sugar

isthmus: a narrow strip of land connecting two larger land masses

lock: a section of a waterway closed off with gates in which vessels in transit are raised or lowered by raising or lowering the water level of that section

mestizo: a person of mixed racial ancestry, especially of mixed European and American Indian blood

mola: a traditional cloth panel stitched onto a blouse by the Kuna Indians containing all types of colorful patterns

nepotism: favoritism shown to one's relatives, usually through hiring practices

oligarchy: a government controlled by a few, especially specific groups or families

paramilitary: a group of civilians organized in military fashion, particularly to operate for a common goal

pipa: a drink made from the sweet milk of unripe coconuts and served in a coconut with a straw

raspado: a flavored snow cone made from shaved ice

smuggler: one who transports something illegally from one place to another through stealth

steam shovel: a large machine used for digging that uses steam as its source of power

CHRONOLOGY

1501
Rodrigo de Bastidas discovers the coast of Panama but is forced to return to Spain.

1502–1503
Christopher Columbus explores the coast of Panama and makes contact with the indigenous tribes. He reports back to Spain that there is gold in Panama.

1509
Diego de Nicuesa is appointed the first governor of Castillo del Oro.

1514
Vasco Núñez de Balboa crosses the isthmus of Panama and discovers the Pacific Ocean. He claims it in the name of Spain.

1514–1527
Pedro Arias Dávila (Pedrarias) reigns as the governor of Castillo del Oro. He is responsible for slaughtering thousands of Indians and for framing Balboa for treason.

1530–1550
The Spanish government builds El Camino Real ("the King's Way") to transport gold plundered and mined throughout Panama and South America.

1572–1596
Sir Francis Drake, an English privateer, loots and plunders Spanish colonies and ships all along the coast of Castillo del Oro.

1717
Panama becomes part of Spanish-controlled New Granada, along with Ecuador, Venezuela, and Colombia.

1821
On November 10 officials from the town of Los Santos are

the first to officially declare Panama's independence from Spain. Too weak and poor to govern as an independent nation, Panama becomes a province of Colombia.

1849
People from all over the United States rush to California in search of gold.

1850–1855
The U.S.-owned Panama Railroad Company builds the first intercontinental railroad across the isthmus of Panama.

1869
The Suez Canal in Egypt is completed.

1881–1889
The French-owned Universal Company of the Interoceanic Canal fails to complete a sea-level canal through Panama.

1903
The United States buys the rights to build a canal in Panama. Panama declares its independence from Colombia on November 3.

1904–1914
The United States builds the Panama Canal, allowing ships to cross through the isthmus.

1932
Harmodio Arias is elected president of Panama and openly opposes an oligarchy.

1952
José Antonio Remon, commander of the National Police in Panama, is elected president.

1964
In a violent display of anti-Americanism, the Flag Riots erupt over one school's refusal to fly Panama's flag alongside the U.S. flag.

1968
Arnulfo Arias is elected president for the third time but is forcefully removed from power by the Panamanian National Guard ten days later.

1969

Omar Torrijos Herrera, leader of the National Guard, rises to power.

1977

Torrijos Herrera signs a treaty with the United States to hand over the Panama Canal to the Panamanian government at the end of 1999.

1981

Torrijos Herrera is killed in a plane crash.

1989

General Manuel Noriega, head of the Panama Defense Forces, becomes head of the Panamanian government with unlimited powers. That same year, the United States invades Panama and forcefully removes Noriega from power, arresting him and imprisoning him in the United States.

1994

Ernesto Perez Balladares becomes the first fully democratically elected president of Panama since Torrijos Herrera took control of the country.

1999

Mireya Moscoso, the widow of Arnulfo Arias, becomes Panama's first female president. That same year, the United States cedes the Panama Canal and all its operations to the Panamanian government.

2003

Panama celebrates its one hundredth anniversary as an independent nation.

For Further Reading

Books

Veronica Chambers, *Marisol and Magdalena: Sound of Our Sisterhood*. New York: Hyperion, 1998. Written for young adult readers, *Marisol and Magdalena* tells the story of two best friends in New York and how one of them deals with separation, boys, new friends, a new language, and a new school when she is sent to live with her grandmother in Panama for a year.

Susan Hassig, *Cultures of the World: Panama*. New York: Marshall Cavendish, 1997. An elementary-level book on Panamanian culture.

Tim McNeese, *The Panama Canal*. San Diego: Lucent Books, 1997. Explores how the Panama Canal was built.

Frederick W. Shaffer, *Mola Designs*. New York: Dover, 1982. Forty-five real *mola* designs made by the Kuna Indians show the texture and variety of this art form.

Judith St. George, *The Panama Canal: Gateway to the World*. New York: Putnam, 1989. A detailed account of the Panama Canal's history for ages ten and up with direct quotes, lots of illustrations, photographs, diagrams, and maps.

Videos

A Man, a Plan, a Canal: Panama. Nova, 1999. A documentary about the history and outcome of a plan to cut a waterway through the Panamanian isthmus, complete with photos, file footage, and firsthand accounts. Narrated by the historian David McCullough, who wrote *A Path Between the Seas.*

WORKS CONSULTED

BOOKS

Tom Barry et al., *Inside Panama: The Essential Guide to Its Politics, Economy, Society, and Environment*. Albuquerque: Resource Center, 1995. A comprehensive look at Panamanian culture with good material on its recent history and societal development.

Kevin Buckley, *Panama: The Whole Story*. New York: Simon and Schuster, 1991. Date-by-date retelling of the Noriega years between 1985 and 1990.

Scott Doggett, *Panama*. Melbourne, Australia: Lonely Planet, 2001. A tour book of Panama with maps, pictures, and tourist information, including some historical background information.

Peter Eltringham et al., *The Rough Guide to Central America*. New York: Penguin Books, 1999. Part of the Rough Guide series, this book deals only in part with Panama.

William Friar, *Adventures in Nature: Panama*. Emeryville, CA: Avalon Travel, 2001. A tour guide of Panama focusing primarily on nature travel, nature-friendly tourism, and eco-tourism.

Diane de Graffenreid, ed., *Panama: Sovereignty for a Land Divided*. Washington, DC: EPICA Task Force, 1976. A short book covering essential Panamanian politics published by the EPICA Task Force in advocacy of the Torrijos-Carter Treaty of 1977.

David Howarth, *Panama: Four Hundred Years of Dreams and Cruelty*. New York: McGraw Hill, 1966. An anecdotal account of Panama's history from the Spanish invasion through the twentieth century.

David McCullough, *The Path Between the Seas: The Creation of the Panama Canal, 1870–1914*. New York: Simon and Schuster, 1977. The most comprehensive book on the history of the building of the Panama Canal.

Alex Perez-Venero, *Before the Five Frontiers: Panama from 1821–1903*. New York: AMS, 1978. This book covers the nineteenth-century history of Panama under Colombian rule in detail.

Karin E. Tice, *Kuna Crafts, Gender, and the Global Economy*. Austin: University of Texas Press, 1995. Accounts and analyses of handicraft production, particularly *mola* making, and the effects on Kuna culture in the twentieth century.

Christopher Ward, *Imperial Panama: Commerce and Conflict in Isthmian America, 1550–1800*. Albuquerque: University of New Mexico Press, 1993. A highly detailed analysis of commerce, demographics, and historical influence during Panama's colonial years.

INTERNET SOURCES

Fellowship of Reconciliation, "Test Tube Republic: Chemical Weapons Tests in Panama and U.S. Responsibility." www.forusa.org.

International Centre for Human Rights and Democratic Development, "Republic of Panama—Act No. 20." www.ichrdd.ca.

Michelle Lescure, "Speaking Out Against Corruption," *World Press Review*, April 11, 2002. www.worldpress.org.

Rob O'Dell, "Drug Trafficking Up in Panama," June 11, 2000, *Cannabis News*. www.cannabisnews.com.

WEB SITES

Amazon Conservation Team (www.ethnobotany.org). This is the Web site of an ecological group that supports biodiversity, culture, and health in tropical America.

Bartleby.com (www.bartleby.com). A research site containing huge amounts of literature and reference resources.

CanalMuseum.com (www.canalmuseum.com). An online museum of the Panama Canal.

Country Studies (http://countrystudies.us). This Web site contains online versions of books previously published by the Federal Research Division of the Library of Congress as part of the Country Studies/Area Handbook series sponsored by the U.S. Department of the Army between 1986 and 1998. Panama is included in the series.

Fellowship of Reconciliation (www.forusa.org). The Web site of the international peace activist group Fellowship of Reconciliation, which includes news and updates on human rights issues in countries throughout the world.

International Reports.net (www.internationalreports.net). An online subsidiary of the *Washington Times* newspaper, providing online news archives from the *Washington Times* in which articles on Panama can be found.

MesoAmerica: Institute for Central American Studies (www.mesoamericaonline.net). A Web site for the institution, which operates language institutes and publishes a regular journal on Central American issues.

Native Planet (www.nativeplanet.org). A Web site that provides information about the Embera and the Wounaan as well as indigenous cultures all over the world and human rights issues.

Panama Canal (www.pancanal.com). The official Web site of the Panama Canal.

The Panama News (www.thepanamanews.com). An online Panamanian newspaper in English.

The Panama Railroad (www.trainweb.org). A Web site that includes information about the history and function of the Panama Railroad.

Panama Women and Children in Need (www.panamawomenandchildreninneed.com). This site contains the text of the "U.S. State Report on Panama."

Panamania.net (www.panamania.net). A large, official site with several different links to interesting features: panoramic virtual reality screens for different places in Panama; a Web cam overlooking the Panama Canal; videos about the history of the Panama Canal (including one with U.S. president Theodore Roosevelt); historical maps; photos of Panama today; lots of history sites; a fun facts page; and even a place to get a free Panama screen saver for your computer.

The Smithsonian Tropical Research Institute (www.stri.org). A good research site about rain forests in the tropics with links to jungle Web cams, maps, and a tree atlas.

U.S. Department of State (http://travel.state.gov). The Web site's "Consular Information Sheet: Panama" contains information for people traveling in Panama.

INDEX

PICTURE CREDITS

ABOUT THE AUTHOR

David M. Armstrong is a graduate of Ohio University in Athens, Ohio. He holds bachelor's degrees in English literature and film production. He currently resides in Japan, teaching English. This is his first publication with Lucent Books.